"This God is our God"

(from Psalm 48:14)

Enjoying the Trinity!

"This God is our God"

(from Psalm 48:14)

Enjoying the Trinity

by

Clifford Pond

Foreword by Gordon Murray

GRACE PUBLICATIONS TRUST
175 Tower Bridge Road
LONDON SE1 2AH

Managing Editors
J.P.Arthur MA
H.J Appleby

ISBN 09464 62 59 3
© Clifford Pond 2000

Distributed by
EVANGELICAL PRESS
Faverdale North Industrial Estate
Darlington
DL3 0PH
England

Printed and bound in Great Britain by Creative Print & Design,
Ebbw Vale, Wales.

Dedication

To all "pew people", with love,
hoping you will read,
understand and profit.

Contents

Foreword

Nothing can be more important for us than to increase in that true knowledge of God which will stimulate faith in him, deepen our love for him and strengthen our resolve to live in holy obedience to him.

Here is an authentically God-centred book that will help believers make appropriate responses to the revelation Scripture gives us of the glory of the Trinity, Father, Son, and Holy Spirit, and its significance for our lives.

May the God of all grace be pleased to use these pages to encourage his redeemed people and move them to heartfelt worship.

Gordon Murray,
(Felixtowe, England)

Introduction

Imagine that you have a valuable Chinese Ming vase, an heirloom handed down to you through many generations. You wrap it up and carefully store it away in a safe place, determined that it will not be damaged or destroyed. Occasionally you remember it is there, so you search it out, dust it off and display it to be admired by you and your family, and perhaps some visitors. Then, after brief exposure, you return it to gather dust again in its place of security. It is so valuable you would hate to lose or damage it, so you give it no daily practical use. This is something like the place the doctrine of the Trinity has in the lives of many Christians. They are sensitive to any damage to it threatened by false teaching, and they would certainly never dream of throwing it away. But it is not something for constant enjoyment or of practical value in the daily struggle of working out the Christian life.

The Psalmist tells us to "Delight yourself in the Lord" (Psalm 37:4). He says he will go "to God, my joy and my delight" (Psalm 43:4). Since God is a triune being, this must mean we are to be thrilled with this aspect of his glory and enjoy a threefold relationship with him. We are to preserve sound teaching about the Trinity, not as we would want to conserve a rare museum piece, but because to neglect this doctrine, and the reality it represents, is to impoverish our spiritual experience and enjoyment of the Christian life.

I shall always be grateful to the Lord for a book of sermons that came my way early in my Christian life. I cannot remember how I came by it or even the name of the author, but I do recall that the title of one sermon in it immediately attracted my attention. It was "The Trinity in Christian experience". I am always suspicious of anything that has no obvious practical value, so that title made sense to me, and so did the sermon. Ever since then I have tried to explore this theme.

What a pleasure it was then, to open Volume 2 of *The Works of John Owen* and discover the first piece, with its full title *of*

Communion with God the Father, Son and Holy Ghost unfolded!
Very long and very wordy, but it repays the effort required to stay
with it. Much shorter, but no less valuable for that, is Donald
Macleod's *Shared Life* with its sub-title *The Trinity and the
fellowship of God's people.*

In his popular *Knowing God* published in 1973, Dr.J.I.Packer
comments:

> The heart of Christian faith in God is the revealed mystery
> of the Trinity ... It is often assumed that the doctrine of the
> Trinity, just because it is mysterious, is a piece of theological
> lumber that we can get on very happily without. Our practice
> certainly seems to reflect this assumption.

Dr. Packer goes on to support this contention by citing the rarity of
sermons on the subject. The Study Guide on his book invites
discussion with the question, "Do you feel the doctrine of the Trinity
is as neglected as Packer says it is?" The answer to that question has
to be, "yes". The Study Guide also asks, "How does the doctrine of
the Trinity make a difference in your own life?" I hope this book
will raise that question for all of us and lead to some fruitful responses.

The neglect of any Christian doctrine has serious consequences
and this is certainly true in the case of the Trinity. I have already
hinted at the impoverishment of our spiritual experience, but that is
not the only casualty. Most of the heretical sects such as Jehovah's
Witnesses or Mormons are what they are because true believers
have neglected some aspect of the Christian faith, and failed to
demonstrate its practical importance. Also, it may well be that failure
to give full weight to the work of the Holy Spirit in earlier years has
been at least partly responsible for the rise of the charismatic
movement. This in turn has led, in many places, to an unbalanced
emphasis on the Holy Spirit. It is a serious mistake either to neglect
or to over emphasise one person of the triune God, because in doing
so we misrepresent God to a needy world.

Another area in which it is important that we keep close to the
Trinity is in the study of world religions. Only people who have lost
a sense of awe and wonder of our God as a Trinity, could possibly

fall for the trite assertion that "all religions are the same", but this is the pressure that is being felt by Christians in western society today.

Issues like this have sounded alarm bells among Christian scholars so that since Packer's book was published, a rash of articles, conference papers and larger works has appeared. In 1983 the British Council of Churches set up a Study Commission on the subject. After five years, this group unanimously agreed that we need to recover the centrality of the doctrine of the Trinity for three reasons: the need to be more biblical in our understanding of God, of worship and of human relationships.

As our book list shows, evangelical scholars have made a large contribution to this discussion, seeking to restore the Trinity to its primary place in our worship and spiritual experience. Many of these writers assert that the history of Christian churches shows that when the Trinity is lost the gospel goes with it. Long ago in the eighteenth century, members of a discussion group of evangelical ministers were saying the same thing:

> One thing struck me in reading Milner's Church History; that in the proportion as the church left the doctrine of the Trinity, it began to lose its life. (R.Cecil)
> The power of vital religion rises or falls with this doctrine. (W.Goode)
> *(The thought of the Evangelical leaders,*
> Editor J.H.Pratt — Banner of Truth)

Stuart Olyott goes so far as to assert:

> A belief in the Trinity is essential to salvation. This does not mean that a believer must understand all the intricacies of this doctrine ... But he must believe that the God who is, is the one revealed in the Holy Scriptures, and that he is one God in three Persons.
> *(The Three Are One*, Evangelical Press)

A recovery of the Trinity at the heart of our faith, prayer life and everyday conduct, is the only adequate defence against the prevailing danger of selling out the distinctiveness of Christianity. Our God, as a triune being, is the pinnacle of our faith — here are splendour, mystery and majesty that dazzle the eye of faith and rebuke our shameful lethargy in praise and adoration to him, and in the proclamation of his greatness to a world that is starved for want of knowing him.

I have not set out to explain the doctrine of the Trinity as such; this has been well done by Stuart Olyott, Donald Macleod and others (see page 156). Rather, my aim is to explore some of the many practical ways in which this doctrine is helpful to us and can be a great blessing to us.

As I begin this work, I am reminding myself that if what I write does not lead me to adoration and submission, then I am missing the mark. Likewise, I hope you will not put the book down without a new song in your heart.

We worship God who has diversity in himself and yet who is one being, totally incapable of division or inner contradiction. It is this amazing unity in diversity that must be reflected in every aspect of church life and in the experience of those who, by faith, "participate in the divine nature" (2 Peter 1:4). This is the glory of God and of our Christian faith.

> Honour, glory, might, and merit
> Thine shall ever be,
> Father, Son and Holy Spirit,
> Blessed Trinity.
> Of the best that thou hast given
> Earth and heaven
> Render thee.
>   (Francis Pott 1832-1909)

God himself, alone, can tell us what he is like. He did not immediately make known that he is three in one at the beginning, but he gradually unfolded this truth about himself in the Scriptures. This process, in itself, is full of practical lessons, and it is where our exploration will begin.

1.
The Trinity and the Bible

We do not read a book of poetry in the same way that we read a novel, nor do we handle a dictionary as we would a biography. Each kind of book makes its own demand on us if we are to benefit from it. The Bible has a character of its own, and because of its size and the variety of its contents it can be very daunting. If only we can discover a key to the understanding of the Bible as a whole, we will know how to handle its various parts. What is this key? It is the fact that everything in the Bible is a gradual unfolding of biblical teaching, like the slow opening up of a rose from its bud.

But how do we know that this is the right key for opening the Scriptures? We know this because it is the very way in which God has told us about himself. He did not immediately try to convince us that he is three persons in one God, but this truth gradually weaves its way through the Bible like a golden thread. If this was God's way in teaching us the most important thing of all, what he is like, we can be sure that this is a very helpful way for us to handle the Bible in all its teaching.

So this is the first practical use we can make of the doctrine of the Trinity. Since the Bible is an account of the way God made himself known as a Trinity, this also teaches us a great deal about the Bible itself and a profitable way for us to study it.

The focal point for our purpose is a moment just before Jesus Christ ascended to heaven. This was when he gave his missionary mandate to his disciples, and as he did so he gave the first full expression to a mystery that had been gradually unfolding throughout human history. When he said that Christian disciples were to be baptised "in the name of the Father and of the Son and of the Holy Spirit" (Matthew 28:19), he was saying something about God that had never before been put into such words. And yet the disciples do not seem to have been surprised. No doubt this was one of the many things Jesus taught them after his resurrection:

> Then he opened their minds so they could understand the Scriptures (Luke 24:45).

Had they not been prepared for it, the disciples would have been startled at the form of words Jesus used. If he had said "in the names of ... " that would still have left open the question of the true nature of the Son and the Holy Spirit. They could have been two more gods, or two lesser beings. But when Jesus said "in the name of ... " he left the disciples and us in no doubt that there is but one being within whom are three, Father, Son and Holy Spirit, and that these three are equally God. They are not three separate beings, or three gods, but three persons in one Godhead.

Jesus was about to ascend to the Father and almost the last thing he did was to tie together the hints, scattered throughout the Scriptures, about the nature of God himself. In fact, although the hints are scattered, there is a clear pattern in the way God has made himself known. It is this pattern that is of special interest to us in this chapter.

One God

From the beginning God made himself known as one — "in the beginning God ... " (Genesis 1:1). This is true despite the attempts of some people to convince us that at the beginning of human history, primitive man in his ignorance adopted the idea of many gods — polytheism — and only later progressed to belief in one God — monotheism. This fitted in very well with the notion that religion can be explained in terms of evolution. But this whole idea is contradicted by the facts, as Ajith Fernando in his *"Jesus and world religions"* says:

> Anthropological studies carried out this century however, have given convincing evidence for the Biblical view, which sees the present religious diversity in terms of the deterioration of an original revelation. Don Richardson has made these insights from anthropology available from a non-technical viewpoint in his "Eternity in their Hearts". He shows how the idea of a supreme, good God was discovered in thousands of primitive cultures that have been studied this century. Richardson relates how these discoveries were embarrassing to many anthropologists because they went against current opinions about the history of religions.

Humans did not progress from polytheism to monotheism, but declined into polytheism from monotheism, as we shall see later.

In the whole of the Bible there is never a time when God speaks and acts in any other way than as one God. This is underlined by the words the Jewish people used as a basic declaration of their faith:

> Hear, O Israel: The Lord our God, the Lord is one (Deuteronomy 6:4).

And yet from the very first verse of the Bible we have hints of something more. The very word used for God in the creation story (Genesis 1:1) is in plural form. As Donald Macleod points out, grammatically it should be translated "Gods":

> The important thing is that when it is used of the God of Israel it has a singular verb or adjective (as if to say, "the Gods is").

Then there are occasions when God speaks of himself in the plural, for example, "then God said, 'Let us make man ...'"(Genesis 1:26) and "Whom shall I send? And who will go for us?" (Isaiah 6:8 see also Genesis 3:22 and 11:7). Alistair McGrath comments that these:

... are usually understood as "plurals of majesty" or "the royal we", although many Christian writers, such as Augustine, argued that these verses already contained hints of a trinitarian way of thinking.

A second Godlike person

As time went on, another godlike person began to come into focus. At quite an early stage he was known as "the angel of the LORD". He appeared as a man or an angel but was quickly honoured and obeyed as God himself. He visited Abraham in his home (Genesis 18:1-15); he surprised Moses by speaking to him out of a burning bush in the desert (Exodus 3:4), and he challenged Joshua as the one who was really in command of the army of Israel (Joshua 5:13-15).

This mysterious person commanded both Moses and Joshua to take off their sandals as reverent recognition that they were in the presence of God. This same person called the unlikely Gideon to lead God's people against their enemies (Judges 6:11). He also called on Samson's parents to tell them of Samson's birth and how they should prepare for it (Judges 13:3). Nor must we forget the fourth person Nebuchadnezzar saw with the three Hebrews in the blazing furnace whom he described as "like a son of the gods" (Daniel 3:25). Isaiah the prophet saw the LORD's glory and this had a profound effect on his whole life (Isaiah 6:1-3); the apostle John tells us that what Isaiah saw was Jesus Christ and his glory (John 12:41).

In addition to this, the Old Testament is strewn with predictions of the future coming of someone special with distinct indications that this person would have godlike qualities. He would be David's LORD as distinct from another whom the Psalmist also calls Lord (Psalm 110:1). He would be Immanuel, meaning "God with us":

> The virgin will be with child and will give birth to a son, and will call him Immanuel (Isaiah 7:14),

and he would be called:

Wonderful Counsellor, Mighty God, Everlasting Father, Prince of peace (Isaiah 9:6).

Of this person it was said "whose origins are from of old, from ancient times" (Micah 5:2), "the man who is close to me! declares the LORD Almighty" (Zechariah 13:7), and indeed "the LORD you are seeking" (Malachi 3:1).

And then he came, as a baby born in Bethlehem named Jesus. His perfect life, his miracles, his death and resurrection all confirmed what the Old Testament had already confirmed, and what he himself claimed: he was and is God.

A third Godlike person

A third godlike person gradually comes to light, who is also mentioned right at the beginning of the Bible and then appears throughout the Old Testament. He is called the "Spirit of God" and he was involved in the process of the creation of the world (Genesis 1:2; see also Job 33:4 and compare this with Psalm 33:6). Later he "came upon" Gideon to strengthen him for his leadership role (Judges 6:34) and much later still, the Lord assured Zerubbabel that his work would be successful "not by might nor by power, but by my Spirit" (Zechariah 4:6). Then there were predictions that this Spirit of God would come into the world. God said to his people in Isaiah's day, "I will pour out my Spirit on your offspring" (Isaiah 44:3). This was confirmed by the prophet Joel and in Ezekiel's ministry. The result would be extraordinary radical changes in the nation and in people's lives:

I will pour out my Spirit on all people. Your sons and daughters will prophesy, your old men will dream dreams, your young men will see visions. Even on my servants, both men and women, I will pour out my Spirit in those days (Joel 2:28-29).

I will sprinkle clean water on you and you will be clean; I
will cleanse you from all your impurities and from all your
idols. I will give you a new heart and put a new spirit in you;
I will remove from you your heart of stone and give you a
heart of flesh. And I will put my Spirit in you and move you
to follow my decrees and be careful to keep my laws (Ezekiel
36:25-27).

Loose ends tied

Such were the "loose ends" that needed to be tied together and this is
precisely what Jesus Christ did. He came with the name "Immanuel"
(Matthew 1:23) and clearly demonstrated that he was the one who
had appeared in Old Testament days and who had been predicted in
such detail.

Gradually, during his ministry, Jesus showed his disciples that
they should call God their Father. While he and the Father were
distinct, they had the closest possible relationship (Matthew 11:27),
and indeed they were essentially one (John 10:30). No threats to kill
him, nor even the crucifixion itself, could make him deny the reality
that he was God in human form (John 10:30-33).

Not only so, Jesus spoke of the Holy Spirit whom he would send:

When the Counsellor comes, whom I will send to you from
the Father, the Spirit of truth who goes out from the Father,
he will testify about me (John 15:26).

and, as we have seen, Jesus clearly indicated that the Holy Spirit is
one both with himself and with the Father (Matthew 28:19).

On the day of Pentecost the Holy Spirit came and fulfilled all
that was predicted of him (Acts 2:14-21). His penetration of people's consciences (Acts 2:37), his transformation of people's lives
(Acts 16:25-34; Galatians 1:23-24) and his causing the spread of
the gospel throughout the world (Acts 17:5-7): all this and more
was nothing less than God himself at work.

This is how God made himself known as Father, Son and Holy Spirit.

Practical Value

What is the practical value of what we have seen about the Trinity so far? Anything that helps us to read the Bible with understanding must be worth our attention, and here there are two great principles for us to follow.

The first is the process we may call "progressive revelation", by which is meant the gradual unfolding of truth from the beginning of the Bible to the end. Some people jump to the conclusion that progressive revelation means progress from wrong ideas to right ones. For example, there is the idea that God in the Old Testament is harsh, cruel and a lover of violence in contrast to a loving, tender, father figure in the New Testament. But this completely ignores much that is said about God in both Testaments. Far from contradicting each other, they provide a remarkably harmonious description of the God we worship. Gradual revelation is not about correcting mistakes or contradictions: rather it is like the alphabet leading the scholar on steadily to a grasp of language. This, then, is the first principle for us to note and act upon. Whatever aspect of God's truth it is that we want to explore, we should try to trace the gradual unfolding of that truth from the beginning.

The second principle is that Jesus Christ himself is the focal point of all God's truth revealed in Scripture. As we read the Bible we will find that every strand of truth has its final and complete demonstration in our Lord Jesus Christ. Our Lord himself put this principle into practice after the resurrection, when he was talking to two people on the Emmaus road:

> … beginning with Moses and all the Prophets, he explained to them what was said in all the Scriptures concerning himself (Luke 24:27).

No matter whether we are thinking about the consequences of sin, the way of salvation, the worship of God, the work of the Holy Spirit, the Christian life or any other aspect of truth, we can trace them through the rituals, history and prophetic ministries of the Old Testament until we come to Jesus Christ in whom all these things have their perfect fulfilment.

> O send Thy Spirit, Lord,
> Now unto me,
> That He may touch my eyes
> And make me see;
> Show me the truth concealed
> Within Thy word,
> And in Thy book revealed,
> I see Thee, Lord.

(Mary A. Lathbury 1842-1913)

2.
The Trinity and persistent love

Nothing could be more practical than teaching which helps us to see the grace of God more clearly, stimulating our love and devotion to him. In this chapter we will look again at the way God made himself known to us as a Trinity, but from a slightly different perspective. As we do so we will see God's grace — his persistent love — in full display.

Sin takes root

We need to go back to the beginning to remind ourselves of the immense problem that had to be overcome — the problem of sin coming into the world through the disobedience of Adam and Eve:

> Therefore, just as sin entered the world through one man, and death through sin, and in this way death came to all men, because all sinned (Romans 5:12, see also Genesis 3).

Sin had terrible universal effects and consequences, and it very rapidly took root in the human race. The most serious consequence was that the knowledge of God became so dim as almost to be blotted out. We are told that:

> The Lord saw how great man's wickedness on the earth had become, and that every inclination of the thoughts of his heart was only evil all the time (Genesis 6:5).

As a result of this, God punished the world with a great flood from which only Noah's family was saved (Genesis 6:5-9:17). Despite this, as the nations developed after the flood they became increasingly godless. We see them building the tower of Babel, apparently in total ignorance of any accountability to God and without any consciousness of him at all (Genesis 11:1-9). God could have left all the people in the dark about himself; they did not deserve any good thing from him, much less a scheme by which people would learn to enjoy fellowship with him. But God's love and sheer undeserved mercy continued to reach out and take the situation in hand.

God reaches out

The question is, how would he, how could he restore the knowledge of himself to people who had become so ignorant of him? As we read the Scriptures, we find that God began the process by calling a man named Abram out of Ur of the Chaldeans and giving him some extraordinary promises:

> I will make you into a great nation and I will bless you; I will make your name great, and you will be a blessing ... and all peoples on earth will be blessed through you (Genesis 12: 2-3).

We know from all that followed, through many centuries until the coming of Jesus Christ, that the greatest blessing that would come to the world would be the knowledge of salvation through God as Father, Son and Holy Spirit. God could, right at the beginning, have informed Abram of the whole truth about himself as a Trinity and expected Abram to understand it, but mercifully that is not what he did. If we, who have the light of the whole Scriptures, have difficulty in grasping this truth, what hope would there have been for people in Abram's day to take it in? So as we have seen, God gradually revealed himself step by step until, at last, Jesus Christ, now alive from death put the whole truth into words:

> Go and make disciples of all nations, baptising them in the
> name of the Father and of the Son and of the Holy Spirit
> (Matthew 28:19).

Returning then to the way God gradually made himself known as
we have seen, he began in the Old Testament by insisting that he is
one God —

> Hear, O Israel: The LORD our God, the LORD is one
> (Deuteronomy 6:4).

God was creating a new nation through which he would make himself
known to the world. That nation, the people of Israel, was surrounded,
almost suffocated, by nations who worshipped many gods
(polytheism). Israel was supposed to be a witness to those nations
that the one and only true God was one God (monotheism) (Isaiah
43: 9-10). This may seem to us to be a simple lesson to learn and we
may wonder why it took so long for further truth to be revealed, but
it proved to be a very hard lesson indeed. The history of the Old
Testament is very largely the story of how the Israelites were more
often influenced by the surrounding nations than those nations
learning anything from the Israelites. The Israelites fell into
polytheism again and again. We see this from the way Joshua
addressed the people just before he died:

> Now fear the Lord and serve him with all faithfulness. Throw
> away the gods your forefathers worshipped beyond the River
> and in Egypt, and serve the Lord. But if serving the Lord
> seems undesirable to you, then choose for yourselves this
> day whom you will serve, whether the gods your forefathers
> served beyond the River, or the gods of the Amorites, in
> whose land you are living. But as for me and my household,
> we will serve the Lord (Joshua 24:14-15).

The Old Testament is the record of a long process of correction and
punishment, and the continual ministry of prophets seeking to purge
the nation of idolatry. Then the Lord spoke to them through Jeremiah:

... though the Lord has sent you all his servants the prophets again and again, you have not listened or paid any attention. They said "Turn now, each of you, from your evil ways and your evil practices, and you can stay in the land the Lord gave to you and your fathers for ever and ever. Do not follow other gods to serve and worship them; do not provoke me to anger with what your hands have made. Then I will not harm you." But you did not listen to me, declares the Lord, and you have provoked me with what your hands have made, and you have brought harm to yourselves (Jeremiah 25:4-7).

The Lord followed this by telling them they would be taken away into captivity by the Babylonians. This happened, and for seventy years they suffered God's chastisement because of their unfaithfulness to him.

At last, when they were released from this captivity, they had become a nation convinced that God is one and that they must worship him to the exclusion of all others. They had learned the lesson.

Then Jesus came

By the time Jesus came into the world this conviction was so fixed in the mind and conscience of the nation that they were completely closed to any further revelation the Lord might give them about himself. It was into this situation that God sent his Son, who step by step demonstrated that he was God in human flesh. The perfection of his life, his extraordinary wisdom and his miracles all confirmed his claim to be the Son of God, by which he meant that he was equal with God. The Jews were in no doubt as to whom Jesus claimed to be but they were unwilling to be persuaded. Having spoken of God as his Father, Jesus said, "I and the Father are one" (John 10:30). This violated their total commitment to God as one, so:

Again the Jews picked up stones to stone him, but Jesus said to them "I have shown you many great miracles from the Father. For which of these do you stone me?" "We are not stoning you for any of these," replied the Jews, "but for blasphemy, because you, a mere man, claim to be God" (John 10:31-33).

Their logic was beyond reproach as they argued that either Jesus was mentally deranged or even demon possessed, or he was who he claimed to be. But the latter was unthinkable to them (John 8:48-59), so in the end they tried to escape their problem by crucifying him.

But the same God who persisted with his Old Testament people despite their spiritual blindness and waywardness did not give up now. He was determined to reveal himself to the world and a way for people to come to him, or else the world would be for ever in darkness. He raised Jesus from death (Acts 2:22-24), and then he sent the Holy Spirit.

… and then the Holy Spirit

Since the Jews generally were so unwilling to receive the revelation that there were the Father and the Son in the Godhead, it is not surprising that our Lord's teaching about the Holy Spirit was largely confined to his ministry to his disciples. Gradually he told them that he must leave them and at the same time he began to introduce the fact that the Holy Spirit would come to them and that he would continue Jesus' presence with them. "I will not leave you as orphans, I will come to you" (John 14:18). Jesus did not suddenly say, Oh, I have something else to tell you; the Holy Spirit is God as well as the Father and myself. But as he explained what the coming of the Holy Spirit would mean to them, he did so in such a way as to leave them in no doubt that the Spirit also is God.

Perhaps the conclusive evidence for this is Jesus's warning of the possibility of blaspheming the Holy Spirit (Mark 3:23-30). It is not possible to blaspheme an angel, a human being or anyone else but God alone. Before he left the disciples Jesus made certain, in many different ways, that they understood that the Holy Spirit was one with him and the Father. Then, as we have seen, after Jesus was crucified and raised from the dead, he brought to a head at last the great truth that in the unity of the being of God there are three distinct persons, so that all true believers are to be baptised "in the name of the Father and of the Son and of the Holy Spirit" (Matthew 28:19). Then, on the day of Pentecost, the Holy Spirit came (Acts 2:1-4). God who had broken into human history when he called Abraham (Genesis 12: 1-2), and in the coming of Jesus Christ into the world (Luke 2: 13-14) now came in the presence and power of the Holy Spirit. A world that did not want to know, was flooded with the full light of the knowledge of God.

Such, very briefly, is the story of how God made himself known in the face of everything that opposed him. We have seen the terrible corruption of the human heart and the blindness and the obstinacy of the human mind, but we have also seen the determination of God to overcome every obstacle. It is difficult to think of anything that could demonstrate the grace of God more clearly than this. The greatest need of men and women is the knowledge of God. Without this, life on earth rapidly becomes full of violence, oppression and corruption, and therefore of pain, misery and hopelessness.

The knowledge of God through Jesus Christ is the only cure for all this now, with eternal life as the supreme blessing (John 17:3).

Triumph of grace

Some people would have us believe that the Bible is the record of people reaching out after God. However, even a superficial reading of Scripture will show that the opposite is true. The Bible is the amazing story of how God defied everything that opposed him in order to give us the most important thing of all, the knowledge of himself.

People generally, have always persuaded themselves that God can be blotted out from their lives, or that they can think out for themselves the kind of god they are prepared to believe in and worship. Nothing has changed. People are the same in their ignorance and self-will, but God's grace is also the same. In amazing love for mankind, he worked steadily against every obstacle until he had inscribed in Scripture the clear evidence of his trinitarian glory.

This is how he deals with us. We are naturally unbelieving, we have no understanding of spiritual things, no sense of our need to know God and no desire to be disturbed in our ignorance. But God's grace is invincible:

> For God, who said, "let light shine out of darkness," made his light shine in our heart to give us the light of the knowledge of the glory of God in the face of Christ (2 Corinthians 4: 6).

His sheer persistence in opening blind eyes and breaking through into human experience should be a constant theme in our praise and worship of our triune God. Not only so, it is our business to show a godless world what God is like. We are to be godly, which among many other things means that we too will persevere in love toward others no matter how obstinate their unbelief may be.

It is surely not surprising that whenever churches have wanted words to express their delight in God on special occasions or in times of special blessing, they have turned to what we call the doxology:

> Praise God, from whom all blessings flow,
> Praise Him, all creatures here below,
> Praise Him above, ye heavenly host,
> Praise Father, Son and Holy Ghost.
> (Thomas Ken 1637 - 1711)

3.
The Trinity and active faith

Twenty-first century people are very suspicious of theories and doctrines. They are all too familiar with scientific theories being contradicted and disproved, and with religious people who believe something quite different from the doctrines they say they hold, or whose lives are quite inconsistent with what they teach. The consequence is that people around us tend to search for practical proof of what is taught; they look for real experience, something they can see working for others and that therefore could work for them.

These attitudes are strengthened by people's reluctance to read. They have a preference for watching television where there is very little straight talking, but a good deal of probing into human experience. The current method of education, in many schools, likewise puts an emphasis on how things work.

When we are faced with new challenges like this, we often discover something to help us in the Bible which we had not noticed before. In our present situation, it is illuminating for us to see that the Bible presents us with a religion of action. We will see this quite clearly as we take a look, from yet another angle, at the way God made himself known to us. Along with the direct teaching in the Bible, he has given us a record of his actions. It was through what he did that he became known. This must be a clue for us as we try to meet the challenge of our day. If God has chosen to make himself known through actions, then this must be a pattern for us to follow.

Clear statements

Immediately we must take care. We must not be so keen to give weight to the working aspect of our faith that we neglect the plain teaching of the Bible, and its many clear doctrinal statements. Some people have gone so far in emphasising the practical nature of Christianity that they have denied that the Bible contains doctrinal statements or clearly stated foundational truths. We have to wonder whether such people have read the Bible, because if they have they would come upon such dogmatic statements as:

I am God Almighty (Genesis 17:1).

The LORD, the LORD, the compassionate and gracious God, slow to anger, abounding in love and faithfulness, maintaining love to thousands, and forgiving wickedness, rebellion and sin (Exodus 34:6-7).

Hear, O Israel; the LORD our God, the LORD is one (Deuteronomy 6:4).

The LORD is righteous in all his ways and loving towards all he has made (Psalm 145:17).

Do you not know? Have you not heard? The LORD is the everlasting God … (Isaiah 40:28).

God is spirit … (John 4:24).

I and the Father are one (John 10:30).

For in Christ all the fulness of the Deity lives in bodily form (Colossians 2:9).

God is love (1 John 4:8, 16).

We must always resist the temptation to say "I can't be bothered with doctrine. I am a practical kind of person. I show my Christianity by my life". If we do not establish ourselves in the teaching of Scripture, we will soon find our faith is undermined by the confused and confusing opinions around us. But, in this chapter we are looking at the opposite mistake of having our heads full of doctrine but without the evidence of the reality of God in our lives.

One important reason why this is a mistake is that it seriously misrepresents our God. There are many things that distinguish

Christianity from other world religions, and one of them is that our
God is a living God, a God of action, the God of the Thessalonian
people who "turned to God from idols to serve the living and true
God" (1 Thessalonians 1:9). The Bible reveals to us the Father, the
Son and the Holy Spirit in and through the great things they have
done and continue to do.

God the Father in action

All God's actions involve all three persons of the Trinity, but we can
distinguish four acts in which the Father is most prominent. The
Scriptures point to each of these as displaying the glory of his
character.

His creation. Again and again the Bible directs our attention to
what God has made in order to teach us what he is like:

> The heavens declare the glory of God; the skies proclaim
> the work of his hands (Psalm 19:1).
> For the LORD is the great God, the great King above all
> gods. In his hand are the depths of the earth, and the moun-
> tain peaks belong to him. The sea is his, for he made it, and
> his hands formed the dry land (Psalm 95:3-5).
> "To whom will you compare me? Or who is my equal?"
> says the Holy One. Lift your eyes and look to the heavens:
> Who created all these? He who brings out the starry host one
> by one, and calls them each by name. Because of his great
> power and mighty strength, not one of them is missing
> (Isaiah 40:25-26).

The evidence of God's wisdom and power in creation is so clear that
Paul is able to say that it is enough to leave people without excuse
for their unbelief (Romans 1:19-20).

His providence. God's providence is his care for the world he has
made, reflecting his love, generosity and compassion. Many of the

Psalms especially celebrate God's goodness seen clearly in action as he provides for the world's needs.

> The LORD is good to all; he has compassion on all he has made (Psalm 145:9 see also Psalm 103:1-6).

The exodus from Egypt. Another great display of God's glory to which the Scriptures frequently point was his deliverance of his people from Egyptian slavery. Immediately after this event Moses and the people sang:

> Who among the gods is like you, O LORD? Who is like you — majestic in holiness, awesome in glory, working wonders? You stretched out your hand and the earth swallowed them. In your unfailing love you will lead the people you have redeemed. In your strength you will guide them to your holy dwelling (Exodus 15:11-13, see also Psalm 66:5-7 and Psalm 136:10-15).

The deliverance from Babylon. Because of their idolatry, God's people were banished into exile in Babylon. As in the case of Egypt, humanly speaking it was impossible for them to be delivered. But God did deliver them and this was seen for generations afterwards as a great demonstration of his glory. In anticipation of this event Isaiah wrote:

> I will make your oppressors eat their own flesh; they will be drunk on their own blood, as with wine. Then all mankind will know that I, the LORD, am your Saviour, your Redeemer, the Mighty One of Jacob (Isaiah 49:26 see also Isaiah 40:3-5 and Ezekiel 39:27-28).

In these and many other ways God showed his people what he is like by demonstrating the truth about himself in his actions. This is how they learned that he is a powerful, holy, caring, merciful and wise God.

Jesus — God in action

The three persons of the Trinity are always in harmony so we would expect the Son and the Holy Spirit also to make themselves known to us in action, giving us an example to follow. Sure enough, they do. In the case of Jesus Christ God's Son, thankfully it is true that there are many clear statements about him in the Scriptures (Isaiah 9:6, Micah 5:2, John 1:1-3, Colossians 1:15-19). Nevertheless, the emphasis is on his actions. His teaching is very important but our faith rests not only on his words but on what he did in his perfect life, his miracles, his death, his resurrection and his ascension into glory.

Jesus himself frequently pointed to his actions. For example, he told the Jews to "believe the miracles" if they would know the truth about him (John 10:37-38). He did the same when John the Baptist sent messengers to ask him to clarify who he was:

> … he replied to the messengers, "Go back and report to John what you have seen and heard: The blind receive sight, the lame walk, those who have leprosy are cured, the deaf hear, the dead are raised, and the good news is preached to the poor" (Luke 7:22).

Jesus also pointed to his crucifixion as the event that would draw people to him (John 12: 32-33).

At the end of his account of the life of Jesus, John reflected on the things that Jesus did and how it was by these that people would know that he was God in human flesh (John 20:30-31) and believe in him. Furthermore the apostle Peter twice directed attention to the life and work of Jesus rather than to his teachings to show who he was (Acts 2:22 and 10:36-38). Once again the lesson is clear that just as the Father and the Son are made known to us by their actions, so our lives too must speak as loudly as, if not louder than, our words.

The Holy Spirit – God at work

The Holy Spirit is also introduced to us primarily in the context of what he does. Our God is a living God! When Jesus told his disciples about the Holy Spirit he said that the Spirit would lead them into the truth; he would convince people of their sinfulness; and he would give them confidence in Jesus Christ himself (John 14:25-26), 15:26-27, and 16:7-11). Jesus did not try to convince his disciples that the Holy Spirit was equal with him in the Godhead, the third person in the Trinity, but he told them what the Holy Spirit would do and they soon drew the conclusion that the Spirit is God in action.

The apostles followed their master in speaking of the Holy Spirit's work. For example, Paul, in Romans chapter 8 shows us the Holy Spirit in action: he controls (verse 9), he leads (verse 14), he testifies (verse 16), and he helps (verse 26).

We can see the Holy Spirit at work in the life and death of our Lord Jesus Christ. The Spirit gave him power to preach effectively:

> The Spirit of the Lord is on me, because he has anointed me to preach good news to the poor ... to proclaim the year of the Lord's favour (Luke 4:18-19).

To perform miracles:

> ... God anointed Jesus of Nazareth with the Holy Spirit and power ... he went around doing good and healing all who were under the power of the devil ... (Acts 10:38).

And to offer himself as a sacrifice for sin:

> ... who through the eternal Spirit offered himself unblemished to God ... (Hebrews 9:14).

The same Holy Spirit gives us the dynamic to live and witness as Christians:

> I pray that out of his glorious riches he may strengthen you with power through his Spirit in your inner being (Ephesians 3:16).

You will receive power when the Holy Spirit comes on you, and you will be my witnesses (Acts 1:8).

Living witnesses

All this is instructive to us. Of course, we must go on preaching and teaching the truths of the gospel, but this must be accompanied by the evidence of God's power in our lives. The way the triune God has made himself known to us is surely to be our pattern; we are made in his image. The people around us must see the truths we are teaching clearly illustrated in the way we live. When Paul wanted to confirm his apostleship to the Thessalonian believers he wrote, "surely you remember, brothers, our toil and hardship ... how holy, righteous and blameless we were among you" (1 Thessalonians 2:9-10). This has always been the right way, but in the unbelieving and very sceptical generation in which we live this principle comes into its own. Our Lord himself laid down the principle in his Sermon on the Mount:

> ... let your light shine before men, that they may see your good deeds and praise your Father in heaven (Matthew 5:16).

The fact that God is active is also a source of encouragement and strengthening for perplexed believers. When we are going through times of spiritual turbulence, we can find help in meditating on what we know of God, his sovereignty, compassion, mercy, holiness, justice and much more. In Scripture God's people were fortified as they recalled past events in which these great attributions of God were demonstrated. A perfect example is the prophet Habakkuk, who was deeply troubled at what was happening to his people — the church of Old Testament times. In the end he was comforted by the recollection of how God revealed himself in the deliverance of the people of Israel from Egyptian slavery and in other great events of Israel's history (Habakkuk 3:3-15).

In times of distress and uncertainty, we too can be encouraged by the great acts of God recorded in Scripture and seen in the history of the Christian church since then. We can be renewed in hope as we read of the power of Jesus Christ changing people's lives, or of the great spiritual revivals that have renewed the churches in their darkest hours.

Holy, holy, holy! Lord God Almighty,
All Thy works shall praise Thy name,
in earth, and sky, and sea;
Holy, holy, holy! merciful and mighty,
God in Three Persons, blessed Trinity!
(Reginald Heber 1783-1826)

4.
The Trinity and fruitful relationships

Communication is one of the distinguishing differences between animals and humans. Some people may want to dispute this, but clearly there is a lot of difference between the built-in routine signals of animals and the creative conversation of human people. We should not be surprised at this, since unlike animals, we are made in God's image. This, among other things, means that we are communicating beings, as God is.

We have discovered all kinds of ways to communicate with one another. Some of these are lamentable, such as physical and verbal violence and deception. We use over-emphasis in such a way that it obscures the truth, and music to condition others into receiving unthinkingly what we say to them. Alas, it is true that sometimes these improper methods have been used by Christian communicators: perhaps sincerely, but none the less mistakenly.

How then, should we set about the task of communicating the gospel in an unbelieving and often hostile environment? This is an important question for all Christians, not only for those involved in preaching and teaching, because we are all called to make the gospel known:

> All you have made will praise you, O Lord; your saints will extol you. They will tell of the glory of your kingdom and speak of your might, so that all men may know of your mighty acts and the glorious splendour of your kingdom (Psalm 145: 10-12, see also Psalm 107:2).

Some people think that we have no need to consider such questions, because all we need to do is to preach the gospel, trusting in the Holy Spirit, and not worrying about how we do it. But if we are obedient to Scripture we will take note not only of the message we have to deliver but also of the method that should be used, especially the example of God himself.

The perfect communicator

As with every question in the Christian life, the starting point for a satisfactory answer must be God himself. We have already seen in chapter three that God communicates the knowledge of himself through what he does. Now we must go on to see that within the very being of God himself there has been throughout eternity the most perfect example of unhindered, unmarred communication. The Father, the Son and the Holy Spirit did not spend unending ages in mutual but mute admiration. They communicated love, contentment and intention one with the other, with not a moment's misunderstanding or disagreement (Matthew 11:27 and 1 Corinthians 2:10-11).

There is an essential unity in all God's activities. As Alister McGrath points out in his *Understanding the Trinity*, God in three persons does not mean that the world is governed by a committee in which divine ideas are discussed and thrashed out, with an occasional casting vote by the Father as chairman. There is an innate harmony in all God's aims, plans and actions, totally unforced, uncontrived and certainly without compromise. Communication between the three persons is perfect, with not a shred of a possibility of crossed lines or misunderstanding. Clearly, if we are to be effective in our endeavours to convey God's truth to the people around us, we need to learn from this perfect example. Since we are made in God's image, it must be a fair assumption that the perfect communication between the three persons of the Trinity should be reflected in our attempts to share the gospel with others.

So, we need to ask what is the secret of this perfect communication. The answer has to be found in the fact of their perfect relationship with each other. Since each of the three is God, and is perfect in wisdom and knowledge, there is no possibility of misunderstanding between them.

God is love

Furthermore, this is a love relationship (1 John 4:16), and there is no doubt that the most effective communication between men and women is also best achieved in the context of a relationship characterised by love. Perhaps it will help us to think of a very imperfect human example. An elderly couple, say John and Joan, have been married for sixty years and more. No doubt in earlier years they had to adjust to one another, overcoming differences of attitude and opinion arising from their differing backgrounds and temperaments. But now, after many years, their understanding of one another is such that they each know instinctively what the other is thinking, and how best to please each other. Now they can communicate messages without even a word being spoken — the raising of an eyebrow, or the movement of a hand will suffice. Long periods of silence are no embarrassment to them. Near perfect understanding and harmony are based on a long standing love relationship.

When the New Testament tells us that "God is love", a moment's thought will convince us that a solitary individual cannot be described as "love". Love is a relationship expressed between persons, so "God is love" must describe an unmarred love relationship within God himself. Donald Macleod put the matter like this:

> Suppose God were not triune. Suppose he had no Son and no Holy Spirit. Whom, then, did he love? How could he be love if there were none to love? We cannot say that he was love because his heart went out towards the world. The world is only of yesterday, God is eternal.

Our problems arise because of our imperfect relationships. We differ from other people in experience, temperament, knowledge and in a host of other ways, and these create hindrances to a meeting of minds. But if we take the Trinity as our example, the solution to our problem has to be in the creation of loving relationships with those we want to win for Christ. When the Proverb says "he who wins souls is wise" (Proverbs 11:30), it could just as well be translated "he who woos souls is wise" — giving us a picture of a developing relationship in love. We can see this marvellously worked out in the way God made himself known to sinful people. There are tremendous impediments to effective communication between the eternal God and created people. The barrier between a holy God and people who were corrupt to the core, could not be penetrated from the human side. How did God set about the task? Did he shout his message or deliver his decrees from his throne high in the heavens? Did he produce a text book, or a work book for people to study and work out the truth for themselves? Thank God he did no such things!

God forms relationships

What he did was first of all to establish a relationship with Abraham and with the nation of Israel that grew from him. This relationship began in earnest with a covenant that was amazingly one-sided. God committed himself to Abraham and his posterity.

> I will make you into a great nation and I will bless you; I will make your name great, and you will be a blessing. I will bless those who bless you, and whoever curses you I will curse; and all peoples on earth will be blessed through you (Genesis 12: 2-3, see also 17: 1-8).

In due time this was followed by God's covenant with Moses, in which he required obedience from the nation and at the same time undertook to fulfil his promises to Abraham. The covenant was sealed with God's oath and with the sprinkling of blood (Exodus 24:3-8 and Deuteronomy 29:12-25). All communication between God and the nation was in the context of a covenant (Exodus 32: 11-14). It was within this relationship that God revealed more of himself, his holiness and his love.

It was also in fulfilment of the terms of the covenant that "God so loved the world that he gave his one and only Son" (John 3:16). This was nothing less than God himself bringing to a head his love relationship with his people by coming and living with them in the person of Jesus Christ. He did not send an angel to convey what he wanted to say, but came as a man amongst men (Hebrews 2: 14-18). The whole idea was that within an on-going relationship between God and his people, they would gradually understand what he was saying to them. This is the lesson we have to learn.

Jesus Christ forms relationships

We are not surprised that Jesus applied the same principles. From the beginning he identified himself with people of all kinds. He spoke human language and lived a human life to the extent that it could be said that he was "tempted in every way, just as we are — yet was without sin" (Hebrews 4: 15). When he wanted to convey his message to his disciples, he did not establish a school that they could attend five days a week. He called them to live with him for three years, so they could not only hear what he said but also see the quality of his life (Mark 3:14). All this took much patience and love, and tested to the utmost his endurance and commitment. He had to bear with this lack of understanding and repeat his teaching over and over again. He had to suffer their earthbound ambitions and foolish self-confidence (Matthew 17:17; John 14:9; Mark 9:33-35; Luke 22:31-34). Furthermore, nothing in this world has been a more effective means of communicating the gospel message than the cross and the sacrifice for sin Jesus offered there. On the cross, loving identification and costly self-giving are perfectly demonstrated.

The Holy Spirit forms relationships

The Father and the Son follow the same pattern, and so does the Holy Spirit. God's ideal method of communication in and through a loving relationship is seen clearly in his way of working also. In perfect harmony with the Father and the Son, the Spirit follows the same principle as he applies the message to human hearts. This is illustrated in the very title Jesus gave to him. He called him "the Counsellor" (John 15:26-27) or "the Comforter" (A.V.) which literally means the one who comes alongside us both to counsel and to strengthen us.

How often we have despaired of someone being converted whom we have prayed for. Perhaps we have tried to work out the best way to penetrate such a person's mind and conscience, only to be frustrated again and again. Sometimes preachers are convinced that a particular message will surely break down the resistance of certain people, but in the event those people are totally unimpressed! Then the breakthrough comes, and to our astonishment it happens in a way we least expect, and a way we would never have thought of using. What has happened? The Holy Spirit, who knows the mind of God, and who knows the human heart, both to perfection, has used the approach that he knew would be perfectly suited to the individual need (1 Corinthians 2:10-14).

Not only so, but he enters into a love relationship with us by taking up residence in our hearts (Romans 8:9). There he continues his great work of transformation. Just as Jesus Christ became a friend of the people, including those who were most despised by others, so the Holy Spirit is willing to enter into a love relationship with people who are corrupted by all manner of evil.

The pattern for us

Here then, are three persons who throughout eternity have been knit together in love and in a perfect harmony of desire and purpose. They communicate perfectly with each other, and with all kinds of people in the world.   Here also, is the pattern for us to have constantly in front of us.

We are not thinking here of the spiritual barrier of sin that blinds peoples' minds; only the Holy Spirit can break it down. Our concern is with the problem of capturing the interest of people around us and of conveying the gospel message to them in a way they can understand. That is to a large extent our responsibility.

The ideal way of trying to communicate the message of the gospel to others, is by first establishing a loving relationship with them. The people we want to speak to differ from us in many ways, such as gender, culture, personality, education, experience and preconceptions. All these and more are hindrances to the clear reception of the message we want to convey to them, and they make it necessary for us to adapt our approach. This includes learning the kind of vocabulary other people are accustomed to using, but it means more than that. It means trying to understand how they think and what "makes them tick". Such harmonisation can only be developed within the kind of relationship we have been considering. This takes time, thought, patience and persistence, but it is worth the effort.

It is true that God can and does at times work more directly and more speedily; he has the right to work as he wills. But what we have seen is his normal pattern and the one he has given us to work by, and it is our responsibility to follow the principles and patterns of Scripture as closely as we can. So when we do this, we will spend time and trouble in forgeing relationships within which mutual love and understanding grow and effective communication becomes possible.

This applies to public speaking as well as to personal witness, and it also applies to writers of Christian literature and to doorstep evangelists. The ideal may not always be possible. For instance, visiting preachers or doorstep evangelists have little opportunity to build up a relationship with the people to whom they talk. Nevertheless, it is usually possible to establish some points of common interest and use these in our approach to them. The same is true of Christian literature where the writer needs to show sympathy with the reader and understanding of his or her situation. Then the reader is more likely to be drawn on to consider the message that follows.

Research into the growth of any church will most often show that behind the success of evangelistic efforts there has been the influence of Christians at a personal level. This should encourage us to persevere in building bridges with unconverted friends. This is the way the triune God works; it is better to follow his pattern than to indulge in methods that arise from human wisdom. In this way we honour him.

God of the covenant — changeless, eternal,
Father, Son, Spirit in blessing agree;
Thine be the glory, our weakness confessing,
Triune Jehovah, we rest upon Thee.
(Jessie F. Webb 1866-1964)

5.
The Trinity and our fragmented world

The past fifty years have seen a rapid disintegration of Western society. Lawlessness, selfishness and apathy dominate the atmosphere while drug addiction, drunkenness and ever more horrifying violence are commonplace. One of the major reasons for this state of affairs is that people generally have lost a sense of the meaning and purpose of life. This in turn is the result of ignorance about our origin and our destiny. The questions, Where did I come from? Why am I here? Where am I going? are, for the most part, not even asked, or if they are, receive confusing or contradictory answers.

"Let us make man in our image" (Genesis 1:26) might well be the most important text as a starting point for the thinking of people today. We have already seen that the fact of our bearing God's image helps us to face the problems of communicating the gospel to others. Now we must consider its application to our understanding of how people should relate to each other in society generally. The image is of a triune God, that is, of a God who is indivisibly one, and yet who is revealed to us in three distinct persons. This is a mystery, not to be understood, but to be received by faith and applied to life as we are guided by the Scriptures.

We need to remember that the entry of sin into the world has marred the image of God in us so that we do not and cannot perfectly reflect that image. But it is not entirely blotted out, and an important part of the effect of the gospel is that God's image is being restored in those who are converted:

... created to be like God in true righteousness and holiness (Ephesians 4:24).

... being renewed in knowledge in the image of its Creator (Colossians 3:10).

The very nature of our God is one of relationship between three persons, Father, Son and Holy Spirit. Since we are made in the image of such a God, we would expect the enjoyment of good relationships to be reflected in human society:

God has created us for relationship, for he is relational. We know that our nature is relational for we do not like being isolated. Loneliness is horrid. The way the human race is structured shows clearly that we are created for relationships. (*The Everlasting God,* D.Broughton Knox)

This immediately lays down a number of guide-lines for the ordering of our society.

Respect

A world that has lost belief in the special creation of humans, soon loses respect for people's lives. It is significant that as soon as we become Christians, we see other people in an entirely different light. This was the experience of the apostle Paul:

So from now on we regard no one from a worldly point of view (2 Corinthians 5:16).

Addressing the Christians of his day, James wrote:

With the tongue we praise our Lord and Father, and with it we curse men, who have been made in God's likeness (James 3:9-10).

The image of God in us requires us that we respect the lives and persons of others. Their reputations should be safe with us, and we must be sensitive to their feelings. The relevance of the gospel could not be more clearly demonstrated.

Community

The image of God is one of fellowship or relationship. Therefore anything that isolates people from each other is contrary to our nature and must be avoided. Where it is unavoidable, its effects need to be recognised and catered for. Increasingly our society is becoming impersonal. We are identified as hands, numbers, or post codes. We pine for the opportunity to deal with people rather than machines such as computers or answer phones. Such pining may betray the age of the writer! Later generations tend to come to terms with the technological age, and indeed to accept it and its consequences as normal. This may be so, but when the consequences are a loss of direct human relationship or the isolation of people from people, we must ask the serious question as to whether such an impersonal society is proper for people made in the image of God.

Some kinds of work, for example night work, tend to isolation and should be reduced to a minimum. There are people who deprive themselves of ordinary community life by so committing themselves to their work or their family that they have no time for relationship with others. Unemployment or redundancy can drive people to the feeling that they are not wanted, which is a kind of enforced isolation. Our social habits are also tending to violate this important principle. Children are increasingly separated from family identity by hiving off to their own rooms to watch television or listen to the radio. The family meal, where all meet, not only to eat but to share news and views, is becoming a rarity. Worse still, children do not find their homes satisfying enough to prevent them from wandering the streets and being led into all kinds of mischief.

But the worst isolation of all is separation from fellowship with God himself. Though they often do not realise it, this is the reason why so many people who do enjoy good human relationships still feel alone in the vastness of the universe. Our God, as a triune being, provides the pattern for a life of fellowship, and for fellowship with himself which we can enjoy even when we are deprived of human companions. The prayer of Augustine expresses this perfectly:

> We were made for you and our hearts are restless until they find their rest in you.

Love

Not only does the Trinity teach us that we are meant to live in relationship with others, but it also underlines that this should be a relationship of love. As we have seen, the fact that "God is love" (1 John 4:16) must mean that the Father, the Son and the Holy Spirit, were committed in love together from all eternity. This is the very nature of God.

One of the worst effects of our sinfulness has been the hindering of harmony between people. This was the very first thing that happened when Adam and Eve disobeyed God and opened the floodgate of sin and its dire effects into the world. Immediately there was a breakdown of the perfect harmony that had existed between them (Genesis 3:11-12). Their conflict was in words, but soon, in their children, it was in terms of physical violence (Genesis 4:1-8).

Even when the situation is favourable to good understanding there is frequently a breakdown on the flimsiest of excuses. But disharmony is even more difficult to avoid when there is prejudice on the basis of class, race, skin colour, sex or religion. This is a shameful disfiguring of the image of God in which we were created. True, humble, self-denying love leading to joy and peace is rare. For the most part we have either mere mutual toleration or increasing aggravation leading to distress, anger and ultimately violence. Churches and individual Christians have a great responsibility to display something of the love relationships that our Creator intended for human society. We will consider this a little further in chapter seventeen.

Love is nothing if it is not practical. A society, conscious of being created by God in his image, will be sensitive to the physical needs of its people. There will be caring and concern at sufficient depth to ensure that no one is deprived of life's basic necessities such as home, food and clothing.

Orderliness

Another characteristic of the life of the Trinity is orderliness. The three persons are equally God and therefore equal in power, wisdom, knowledge and every other attribute. Yet each has his place and that place is not usurped by the others. For example, neither the Father nor the Holy Spirit was crucified for our salvation. There is order: the Son is eternally derived from the Father, and the Holy Spirit is eternally going out from the Father and the Son. This is completely beyond our understanding, we cannot begin to get near it, but this much is clear, our God in his very nature is a God of order. It is also clear that society composed of people made in God's image is meant to be orderly, and that where there is confusion and chaos it is a slight on the name of our Creator. Anarchy — lawlessness — is not merely to be regarded as a bad thing according to human reason and experience; it is to be seen as violating God's original design and is therefore the high road to self-destruction.

This has a considerable bearing on some other matters that all too often agitate and even aggravate human relationships. There is frequently a questioning of the roles different people play in society and this can spill over into an actual rebellion against authority. What right have governments, employers, magistrates, church leaders, parents or husbands to assume the leadership roles that traditionally have been given them? We cannot here examine these situations in detail, each of them is worth treatment in many books. But there is a basic principle that should undergird all of them. The principle is this; just as there is order in the being of our Creator in whose image we are made, but that order does not imply inequality or any kind of inferiority, so society must be ordered in such a way as to recognise and honour the equality and dignity of all people.

To state this principle another way; just as there is both diversity and unity in the Godhead, so there should be both diversity and unity in human society. This means, for example, that we should be submissive to the state, but the state must not use us as pawns in a struggle for political power. Or, again, while teachers and parents have positions of responsibility, children are to be treated with respect and justice. Prison officers must control prisoners but not regard them as inferiors. Wives and husbands have different roles to play in family life, but neither is to treat the other as of lesser importance or usefulness. Employers have a responsibility to make their business prosperous but not at the expense of the dignity of their employees, each of whom has specific gifts and is to be valued. Everyone in this world should be made to feel valued.

Diversity

Within the Trinity there is both unity and diversity, and ideally this is to be reflected in human society. There are two opposite mistakes we can make. We can so emphasise the idea of unity and equality, and the need for a "classless society" that people become almost like mass-produced products. This has been seen in some communist countries; when their leaders appear on television screens they tend to be expressionless look-alikes. On the other hand we can so underline diversity that people become proud of their abilities, their homes or their class. Some people are snobbish, exaggerating their own importance and despising what they consider to be the lesser gifts of others. They must learn to humble themselves and to realise that they are what they are only because of the goodness of God to them. They have nothing to boast about except their responsibility to serve others and to make it possible for them also to be useful citizens.

Other people feel that they are of no use, and have nothing to contribute to family or community life. None of us must have any illusions about our acceptability to God. There is nothing in any of us that is good enough to please him. But we are human beings and no matter whether we are Christians or not, we are made in God's image and for this reason we should have a sense of self-worth. Our talents and abilities may be very modest, but whoever we are and whatever our gifts, there is a place of usefulness for each of us in God's world.

The church is often considered to be of no importance and its message is thought to be irrelevant in modern society. If we insist on teaching the doctrines of the Christian faith, we are sometimes seen as people beating the air to no purpose and indulging in meaningless speculation. As for the doctrine of the Trinity, people generally see no point in it at all. But here we have seen that nothing could be more relevant or more practical than to restore the Trinity to a large place in our thinking, and to work out what it means for us to be made in the likeness of such a God. These things will be worked out in a much fuller way in the churches when the members are "born again". We will see this in chapter seventeen. Nevertheless, the example of the churches and their witness to the triune God, will have a wholesome, healing influence on an unregenerate society.

We go to a fragmented world with a book — the Bible — that is rich in both the diversity and the unity of its message. Society is fragmented because individuals are mixed-up and confused in themselves. The book itself, is a perfect illustration of its own account of a God who is able to give wholeness both to individual people and to society itself.

Holy, holy, holy! all
Heaven's triumphant choirs shall sing,
When the ransomed nations fall
At the footstool of their king:
Then shall saints and seraphim,
Harps and voices, swell one hymn,
Blending in sublime accord,
Holy, holy, holy Lord!

(James Montgomery 1771 - 1854)

6.
The Trinity and the gospel message

The world needs the gospel, but what has the doctrine of the Trinity to do with evangelism? Surely, if we bring the Trinity into our gospel preaching we will bore and bemuse people, and obscure the simplicity of the message. But in this, as in everything else, we must be guided by Scripture, and if we are, then the Trinity will give structure and content to our evangelism.

There is no evidence that the early preachers set out to explain the doctrine of the Trinity when introducing people to the gospel. It is doubtful even if this was done after people were converted, because the doctrine itself was not formulated in the way we know it today until the fourth century A.D. However, we cannot leave the matter there, because we have to remember that our Lord instructed the apostles to:

> make disciples ... baptising them in the name of the Father and the Son and the Holy Spirit (Matthew 28:19).

Imagine the situation on the day of Pentecost, at Caesarea or at Philippi. The gospel message has been preached, people have responded, and now they are baptised. The question has to be asked; When the apostles baptised them "in the name of the Father and of the Son and of the Holy Spirit", did Lydia in Philippi, for example, know what they were talking about? Did she think it was some kind of magical or mystical formula adding nothing to her enjoyment or to the significance of her baptism?

The answer to this question must surely be that Lydia, and others like her, did have some notion as to what those words meant, and that they had practical value for her at the time of her commitment to Christ. The gospel message had been presented to her in such a manner that the words used at her baptism harmonised with that message. She did not fully grasp the glorious truth about the God to whom she was now reconciled, any more than others at that time, but she did know that now she was united by faith to God who was presented to her as Father, Son and Holy Spirit.

In chapter eight we will discuss in more detail the practical value of knowing God as three persons when we are baptised. Our purpose here is to look a little further into the way the apostles presented the gospel so that the words they used at the baptism of believers did not come as a shock, surprise or mystery to them. Perhaps the best way to approach this is to notice two mistakes that it is possible for gospel preachers to make.

Two possible mistakes

The first mistake is to present Jesus Christ almost, if not entirely, to the exclusion of the Father and the Holy Spirit. Most often this approach is justified by reference to Paul's words "I resolved to know nothing while I was with you except Jesus Christ and him crucified" (1 Corinthians 2:2). The argument claims that Paul realised he had made a mistake at Athens when he preached on Mars Hill (Acts 17:22 - 31). That sermon is said to be philosophical and lacking in a cross-centred message. We will deal with that argument in a moment, but for now we must notice the dangers involved. It is possible to preach Christ crucified in such a way that people have little idea that through what Jesus suffered on the cross they are reconciled to a holy God. Also, salvation from the penalty of sin through Christ crucified tends to be isolated from the gospel demand of a changed life made possible by the Holy Spirit. To such people the trinitarian declaration in baptism is likely to be only empty words.

The second mistake is for evangelists to dwell on the transforming work of the Spirit, with inadequate reference to the Father and the Son. The danger here is that people are able to give testimony to a tremendous change in their lives, but without any experience of a sense of guilt and fear of God's judgement. Their talk is of being changed but not of being saved. Once again the trinitarian form of the baptismal commission has little meaning beyond being very nice religious words.

The answer to our enquiry must be that the apostles so preached that the words "Father, Son and Holy Spirit" made sense to those baptised. Clearly we must try to do the same, but what does this imply?

Beginning with God

Let us now return to the arguments based on Paul's words "I resolved to know nothing while I was with you except Jesus Christ and him crucified". It is quite gratuitous to suggest that Paul thought his sermon at Athens was a failure and therefore a mistake because of the apparently poor response to it. We should be glad that people do not judge our sermons today on that basis. We do not know a great deal of what happened in Athens after Paul's visit, but we do know that a church was founded there and that it survived right into the fourth century. In the meantime it was strong enough to produce some outstanding leaders and teachers.

Paul's Mars Hill sermon was consistent with a pattern that is clear for all to see in the New Testament. When the apostles addressed Jews, or reasoned with them, the emphasis was on showing from the Old Testament Scriptures that Jesus was the promised one — the Messiah (Acts 13: 14-41, 17: 1-4). The Jews did not need to be convinced that they were made by the one true God and were accountable to him. They were well aware of that. But when the apostles were dealing with people with no Old Testament in their hands or hearts, then their approach was entirely different. They began, not with Scripture, but with the common ground of creation and human preconceptions. What they said was entirely consistent with the Old Testament, and indeed flowed out from that revelation. Also, the good news they proclaimed was centred in Jesus Christ crucified, but it took them a little longer to reach that point than when they were addressing Jews.

We see then, that to restrict gospel preaching simply to Christ crucified is not in harmony with the practice of the apostles. Furthermore, a careful thought about what Paul wrote will show what he meant. He wrote:

> When I came to you, brothers, I did not come with eloquence or superior wisdom as I proclaimed to you the testimony about God. For I resolved to know nothing while I was with you except Jesus Christ and him crucified (1 Corinthians 2:1-2).

The context of "Christ and him crucified" was Paul's "testimony about God" and this is consistent with his frequent use of the expression "the gospel of God" (Romans 1:1, and 15:16, 2 Corinthians 11:7, and 1 Thessalonians 2: 8 & 9; see also 1 Peter 4:17).

Nor is this all. Paul went on to remind the Corinthian believers that the Holy Spirit was at work among them as the message was preached (1 Corinthians 2:4-5). By the power of the Spirit, minds and hearts were opened to love for Jesus Christ and faith in him, and lives were transformed. Did all this happen without Paul explaining to them that it was the Holy Spirit who had begun his work in them? I doubt that very much!

Gospel preaching

So we conclude, as we have already said, that the apostles preached the gospel in such a way that their converts were aware of the Father, the Son and the Holy Spirit, and they knew the significance of being baptised in the name of the Trinity. When we follow their example, we ensure that people are left in no doubt that they stand condemned before God. The sacrifice of Christ is not presented only in terms of love, but as the only means of reconciliation to God. Also, the work of the Holy Spirit is not seen in isolation from a deep awareness of sinfulness and the need to trust in Jesus Christ alone for deliverance from the wrath to come.

This would suggest a logical order in the presentation of the gospel: the condemnation of a holy God, the way of forgiveness through Jesus Christ and then the power of the Holy Spirit to give life, faith and enabling to live in a godly manner. That would be right, and in modern western society this may well be the best pattern to shape our gospel preaching.

Another reason why this should be our emphasis in these days is that the prevailing practice among evangelicals majors on the life changing power of the Holy Spirit. All too often, at the same time, little attention is given to the need for repentance before God and faith in Jesus Christ as the only Saviour from sin and its eternal consequences. But the emphasis in the Bible is on the need for repentance and faith, as a reading of the first three chapters of Paul's letter to the Romans shows.

Quoting from Psalm 36, the apostle Paul summarised the state of the world in general, "there is no fear of God before their eyes" (Romans 3:18). We will agree that those words are an accurate description of the world around us today. In this situation it may well be that our emphasis should be on sin against a God whom people do not fear, and reconciliation through Jesus Christ to a God they do not recognise. On Mars Hill, Paul addressed people like that, and for them he began his gospel with the fact of God as the Creator and the one to whom we all must give account.

However, it would be wrong to put ourselves into a fixed mould and be inflexible in our approach. Our Lord and his apostles always adapted their style of presentation to the culture, experience and specific needs of their hearers. When we bear this in mind, we see how wonderfully helpful the fact of the Trinity is in practice. I have no wish to encourage new moulds of rigid practice, but we can illustrate the flexibility the Trinity gives us in this way:

- 1. Begin with God the Father — with those who have no notion of their need as sinful and condemned persons.
- 2. Begin with God the Son — with those who have some feeling of guilt.
- 3. Begin with God the Holy Spirit — with those whose lives are ruined by corrupt practices.

It is obvious that there are endless variations on this theme. For example, the cross of Christ can be used to press home people's sinfulness and guilt before a holy God. We must avoid rigidity and not create new strait jackets.

The important issue here is to make sure that in the end we are being trinitarian. Whatever our starting point, the finishing place in our evangelism must be total, exclusive, sin-renouncing faith in Jesus Christ alone, leading to peace with God and a changed life through the presence of the Holy Spirit. This is not to say that every message has to be totally trinitarian. Not at all! But it does mean that when someone is baptised in "the name of the Father and of the Son and of the Holy Spirit" they know what this means and the benefits and blessings these words embrace. As someone has said "the Trinity is the gospel and the gospel is the Trinity".

> Thank You, O my Father
> for giving us Your Son,
> and leaving Your Spirit
> till the work on earth is done.
>   (Melody Green)

7.
The Trinity and salvation

The spiritual experience of many professing Christians is rather deficient. Their hearts are not ringing with joyful thanksgiving. Their singing of hymns of exaltation and praise is matter-of-fact and without feelings of thrill or excitement. One reason for this is that they have a low view of what salvation is, and of the amazing thing that has happened to them to deliver them from sin and its consequences. Occasionally they are stirred by reminders of the sufferings of Jesus and the terrible price he paid for their redemption, but such emotions ebb and flow. Another means of prompting some heartfelt praise is the realisation of their total unworthiness of God's mercy. Sometimes the meaning of God's grace is explained as "**G**od's **R**iches **A**t **C**hrist's **E**xpense" — or as the unmerited favour of God, and these thoughts provoke feelings of gratitude and love. However, it is noteworthy how frequently in the New Testament, when the apostles gave themselves to expressions of sheer delight, these had an even more profound origin. They arose from a contemplation of the involvement of the three persons of the Trinity in the whole process of our salvation. The most outstanding example of this is in Paul's letter to the Ephesians (1: 3-14). We will explore these verses later (chapter 11) but we turn here to another passage from Paul and one from the apostle Peter.

2 Thessalonians 2: 13-14

> But we ought always to thank God for you, you brothers
> loved by the Lord, because from the beginning God chose
> you to be saved through the sanctifying work of the Spirit
> and through belief in the truth. He called you to this through
> our gospel, that you might share in the glory of our Lord
> Jesus Christ.

We are immediately impressed by Paul's concentration on what God
has done for us. If we dwell more on what we have done, or even
what we have been enabled to do, our sense of thankfulness and
praise will be impoverished.

The first and most astounding thing is that God has loved us.
Why should a sovereign, holy and just God even take notice of us?
Why should he not only take notice of us but love us despite all the
corruption he sees? Those questions will probably go forever unan-
swered. The words recall the blessing of Moses on the tribe of
Benjamin "let the beloved of the Lord rest secure in him" (Deuteronomy 33:12), and the assurance given to God's undeserving people
through the prophet Jeremiah, "I have loved you with an everlasting
love; I have drawn you with loving-kindness" (Jeremiah 31:3).

Even more remarkably, our Lord himself has revealed the measure of our Father's love for us. In his prayer, recorded in John 17, he
likened the Father's love for his people to his love for Jesus himself:

> ... you ... have loved them even as you have loved me
> (John 17:23).

There is surely nothing more amazing than this among all the astounding things we find in Scripture. The Father loved the Son
eternally, perfectly and without hindrance or hesitation. That is how
he loves us. Can you believe it? This being so, what shall we say
about the next thing, that this God chose us to be saved "from the
beginning"?

Chosen to be saved

Some people are thrilled to discover that their family history can be traced back many centuries and has links with the rich or famous. This is nothing compared with the knowledge that we were in the loving purpose of the eternal God "from the beginning". We can judge what Paul meant by "in the beginning" from his words to Timothy, "This grace was given us in Christ Jesus before the beginning of time" (2 Timothy 1:9). God's purpose was to save us. This includes rescuing us from his wrath and his just condemnation of us, reconciling us to himself, pardoning our sins and beginning a work of restoration within us.

The work of the Holy Spirit

How is this salvation made real to us? The answer is that the Holy Spirit takes hold of us, marks us out as belonging to God (sanctification), and leads us to believe the gospel. This is what Paul meant when he wrote that we were all "baptised by one Spirit into one body" (1 Corinthians 12:13).

We should never underestimate the tremendous nature of what has happened to us. We will make this mistake if we forget our awful spiritual state before the Holy Spirit began his work in us. We were unholy people, corrupt in mind and heart; we were blind, often wilfully blind to the truth; we were obstinately opposed to God and hardened in unbelief. No-one other than God himself in the person of the Holy Spirit has enough wisdom, enough power, and enough love to turn us around and make us willing for holiness.

Through the gospel

Nor is this the whole story, because Paul tells us that the Holy Spirit uses the gospel to achieve his purpose. This gospel is none other than the good news about Jesus Christ, God's Son, coming into the world for our salvation. The Holy Spirit shows us that when Jesus Christ died, he was taking the place of sinful people. He took their guilt and so he endured the just punishment of their sins. He died in their place, was buried and then was raised to life again. His resurrection was the proof that God had accepted his sacrifice on their behalf:

> He was delivered over to death for our sins and was raised to life for our justification (acceptance with God) (Romans 4:25).

And then the final stage in God's purpose of love is the ultimate sharing of the glory of Jesus Christ in God's presence, as Jesus himself prayed:

> Father, I want those you have given me to be with me where I am, and to see my glory (John 17:24).

Why did Paul write like this? His purpose was to strengthen true believers against the heresies and apostasy that would pervade the world (2 Thessalonians 2:1-12). So he follows the reminder of the glory of their salvation with the exhortation:

> So then, brothers, stand firm and hold to the teachings we passed on to you, whether by word of mouth or by letter. May our Lord Jesus Christ himself and God our Father ... encourage your hearts and strengthen you ... (2 Thessalonians 2: 15-17).

1 Peter 1:1-2

This trinitarian understanding of our salvation is not confined to the teaching of Paul. Peter expresses it in a slightly different way, and in so doing develops our understanding of what our salvation involved.

Peter's purpose again is to comfort and strengthen Christian believers who were no longer "at home" in the world and who were suffering for their faith (1 Peter 4:12). He does this by reminding them of the glory of the gospel and the deep roots of their salvation:

> ... chosen according to the foreknowledge of God the Father, by the sanctifying work of the Spirit, for obedience to Jesus Christ and sprinkling by his blood (1 Peter 1:2).

"Chosen according to the foreknowledge of God" (see also Romans 8:29) reminds us that not only is our salvation rooted in eternity, but also that it had its origin in the heart of God. "Foreknowledge" means more than God's advanced knowledge of us and what he would do for us. It is the knowledge of intimate love; the Father set his love upon us before he created the world.

The Spirit was in complete harmony with the mind of the Father, so that, as we have seen, at the appropriate time, he began his work of grace in us.

Obedience to Jesus Christ

This work of grace leads us to "obedience to Jesus Christ", which means submission to Jesus Christ as our Lord. This is the reverse of our modern habit of urging people to trust in Jesus Christ as their Saviour, and after that to yield themselves to him as their Lord. The Spirit's work first brings us to a position of humility before Jesus as our Master. It is as our Lord that he commands us to follow him and believe in him (Acts 9: 1-6). This, in turn, leads us to all the benefits Jesus Christ gained for us through his death on the cross. The words "sprinkling by his blood" take us back to the occasion when Moses sprinkled the blood of young bulls on the people of Israel (Exodus 24:4-8). This symbolised their receiving of the pardon and reconciliation to God that had been secured for them by the sacrifice of those animals.

More than this, the blood of the Old Testament sacrifices united those people to the covenant of God. Jesus referred to this when he instituted the Lord's supper; as he served the wine he said:

This is my blood of the covenant which is poured out for many for the forgiveness of sins (Matthew 26:28).

The writer to the Hebrews described this as "the blood of the eternal covenant" (Hebrews 13:20) which guarantees forgiveness for all who are led by the Spirit to trust in Jesus Christ.

So we see that our salvation is the work of the three persons of the Trinity acting in perfect harmony. The Father's electing love is matched by the self-giving and suffering of the Son, which in turn is matched by the powerful work of the Spirit in the hearts of rebellious people.

Here is the way the Bible stimulates our praise to God and joy in him. It is not by the artificial stirring of our emotions by endless singing or any other psychological manipulation, but by reminding us of the length, breadth, depth and height of our salvation.

Three Persons and one God, I bless and praise thee,
   for love so unmerited, so unspeakable, so wondrous,
   so mighty to save the lost and raise them to glory.
O Father, I thank thee that in fullness of grace
   thou hast given me to Jesus,
   to be his sheep, jewel, portion;
O Jesus, I thank thee that in fullness of grace
   thou hast accepted, espoused, bound me;
O Holy Spirit, I thank thee that in the fullness of grace
   thou hast exhibited Jesus as my salvation,
     implanted faith within me,
     subdued my stubborn heart,
     made me one with him for ever.
             (*The Valley of Vision* Banner of Truth)

The Grace of God

We often define God's grace as his undeserved favour. In the light of what we have seen in this chapter, perhaps we can open that up like this:

It is the love, wisdom and power of God the Father, the love, wisdom and power of God the Son, and the love, wisdom and power of God the Holy Spirit, working in perfect harmony to bring a countless number of ill-deserving people from spiritual death to life and from the power of Satan to God, guaranteeing their ultimate sharing of the glory of Christ.

> Hallelujah! Hallelujah!
> Glory be to God on high;
> To the Father, and the Saviour,
> Who has gained the victory;
> Glory to the Holy Spirit,
> Fount of love and sanctity,
> Hallelujah! Hallelujah!
> To the Triune Majesty.
>
> (W.C.Dix 1837 - 98)

8.
The Trinity and Believers' Baptism

Baptism, immersion in water, as a public declaration of our faith in Jesus Christ, is a great event in a believer's life. A clear understanding of its meaning makes it an even more memorable occasion. We understand believers' baptism to be an act of obedience to Jesus Christ our Lord. His great commission leaves us in no doubt about this:

> Therefore go and make disciples of all nations, baptising them in the name of the Father and of the Son and of the Holy Spirit (Matthew 28:19).

As we obey this command we are doing many other things. We are making a declaration of our faith in the Lord Jesus Christ as our Saviour from sin and its consequences. We are identifying ourselves with him in his death, burial and resurrection, symbolised by our immersion in water (Romans 6:4). We are also submitting ourselves to Jesus Christ as Lord and recognising his right to rule over our lives. All these things are right and their importance must not in any way be minimised. But if we read the text again we will see that there is more yet to believers' baptism. There is also a trinitarian dimension that can be highly significant for us.

Our Lord's words here have caused some questioning. His clear statement of the Trinity seems to come so suddenly that some people have even doubted that Jesus actually spoke them, suggesting that they were added at a later time when understanding of the doctrine was more fully developed. But the evidence of the existing New

Testament documents is consistent with attributing these words to Jesus. Furthermore, as we have seen in chapters 1-3, he had prepared the way for this statement by his many references to the Father and the Holy Spirit.

We may also recall that there had already been a trinitarian dimension to our Lord's own baptism:

> As soon as Jesus was baptised, he went up out of the water. At that moment heaven was opened, and he saw the Spirit of God descending like a dove and lighting on him. And a voice from heaven said, "This is my Son, whom I love; with him I am well pleased" (Matthew 3: 16-17).

Undoubtedly the baptism of Jesus has a significance which ours does not. He, the sinless one, was identifying himself with sinful people, and committing himself to suffer the guilt and punishment of their sins. We can have no part in that wonderful saving ministry.

Our Lord's baptism and ours

Nevertheless, we would surely be surprised if there were no connection between Jesus' baptism and ours. There must be reflections of the one in the other. For example, just as his baptism was a commitment to his task, so in our baptism, we are giving ourselves to the Lord, to his service and to the spread of the gospel.

And then, consider the words of the Father. We know little of our Lord's early life up to his baptism, but in these words the Father assured his Son and everyone else, that he had been faultless and totally pleasing to him. Of course, there is no way that our baptism could celebrate any kind of perfection in us — the opposite is true! But there is a positive sense in which our baptism does celebrate our acceptance with God because of our union with Christ and his perfection being accredited to us. The Father sees us "in Christ", and because of this, he says to us "You are my child and I am well pleased with you".

In addition to all this, the descent of the Holy Spirit on Jesus is also mirrored in our baptism. On the day of Pentecost, Peter commanded the new believers:

> Repent and be baptised, every one of you, in the name of Jesus Christ so that your sins may be forgiven. And you will receive the gift of the Holy Spirit (Acts 2:38).

For Jesus, this was the outpouring of the Spirit upon him for the work to which he was committed, and the same Spirit is promised to us at our baptism. Christian teachers differ in their understanding of this promise. Clearly it is not the same as regeneration by the Spirit, which must precede believers' baptism. The promise does indicate a gracious blessing from the Lord and it may be that this varies from believer to believer, according to need. It may take the form of enhanced assurance of salvation, or a sense of the Lord's commissioning for his work, or some other spiritual benefit. The Spirit strengthens us for the life of holiness we are called to live, and the specific work the Lord gives us to do.

These are some of the ways in which our Lord's baptism and ours run parallel to each other. Now let us consider what more the trinitarian dimension in believers' baptism can mean for us.

We have already seen that when the disciples baptised people like the Ethiopian eunuch (Acts 8:26-39) or the Philippian jailer (Acts 16:22-34) they would have used the name of the Trinity as our Lord commanded; so the eunuch and the jailer must have had some idea what those words signified. This is clear from an incident in Ephesus when Paul visited the city. He met some dozen professed disciples, whose understanding and experience did not measure up to their being true Christian believers. He asked them:

> "Did you receive the Holy Spirit when you believed?" They answered, "No, we have not even heard that there is a Holy Spirit." So Paul asked, "Then what baptism did you receive?" "John's baptism," they replied. Paul said, "John's baptism was a baptism of repentance. He told the people to believe

in the one coming after him, that is, in Jesus." On hearing this, they were baptised into the name of the Lord Jesus (Acts 19:2-5).

They had been baptised, but that was not Christian baptism because they had not even heard of the Holy Spirit. Also, it would seem they did not have a clear understanding of the Lord Jesus Christ. Consequently, Paul regarded their baptism as deficient of a trinitarian dimension, so they were "re-baptised". The fact that this was "into the name of the Lord Jesus" does not imply that there was no trinitarian reference. It simply emphasises that this was a Christian baptism rather than John the Baptist's.

It is not possible that those early believers would have had any deep understanding of something that took centuries for Christian teachers to clarify. But they knew enough for the words not to be meaningless. Our understanding of the Trinity is certainly still very limited, but this great truth can mean more to us than to those early believers, since we have the benefit of the writings of the apostles in the New Testament to guide us.

In, or into the name

There is a debate among scholars as to whether the translation should be "in the name ... " or "into the name ... " It would be inappropriate for us to discuss this here, much less to presume to express our opinion either way. However, there is no doubt about the significance of "the name". This means more than baptism being conducted at the command of God or under his authority. This is true, but "the name" in Scripture has a much deeper meaning, involving the person and character of the one named. This is clear in these quotations from the Old Testament:

Those who know your name will trust in you (Psalm 9:10).
Sing to God, sing praise to his name (Psalm 68:4).
The name of the LORD is a strong tower; the righteous run to it and are safe (Proverbs 18:10).

It is obvious in these verses that "the name" means more than a mere identification of the person, and that it reflects the trustworthiness, strength and greatness of God. So when we are baptised "in the name of the Father and of the Son and of the Holy Spirit", we are demonstrating our identification with each person of the Trinity and expressing our love for them and our confidence in them and all they have done for us and continue to do for us. All that we know of the work of grace (described in chapter 7) at the time of our conversion, whether little or much, can be poured into our understanding of baptism, immensely increasing the joyful experience of that occasion. Answering the question, "What is signified in baptism?" James B.Torrance wrote:

> It is a sign of the one work of the one God, Father, Son and Holy Spirit in the fulfilment of his filial purpose "to bring many sons to glory". Why do we baptise in the triune Name? Not just because of our Lord's missionary command in Matthew 28:19, but because these words enshrine the good news of grace. (*Worship, Community, and the Triune God of Grace*)

Qualifications for believers' baptism and church membership

There have been times in the history of believers' baptism when churches have laid down such strict conditions for baptism and church membership that few people dared to present themselves for acceptance. Such churches required people to have a grasp of the whole range of theology and to have certain prescribed spiritual experiences before they were approved.

It was very necessary for that kind of thing to be corrected; but as so often happens, in recent years the correction has gone too far. In all too many places, little is expected by way of understanding sound doctrine. The effect of this is that baptism and church membership lack a depth of meaning, and in consequence there is less sense of wonder, awe and privilege than there can be and should be.

This is not to plead for the erection of new barriers. Nor is it to ignore the simplicity and immediacy of the baptisms of believers recorded in the New Testament. But it does mean the restoration of baptism as an occasion to be treasured and remembered throughout the lives of Christian believers. A recovery of the trinitarian dimension in believers' baptism will surely help to achieve such desirable aims.

Two further comments are relevant. We have seen in chapter six that people in the western world generally have lost the sense of a "fear of God". Because of this, our evangelism needs to have a clear emphasis on the glory and majesty of God, on our accountability to him, and on our need to be reconciled to him through Jesus Christ and our lives changed by the Holy Spirit.If we do this, then believers' baptism will be seen as a commitment to God in three persons. If the people around us think of God at all, their ideas of him are mistaken and most of them amount to a very feeble inadequate being. In this context believers' baptism becomes a declaration of faith in the one "living and true God" (1 Thessalonians 1:10), glorious in the mystery of triune holiness, power and love.

The second comment bears on the lamentable fact that all too many people, once baptised, defect from faith in Jesus Christ. Perhaps if we took more trouble to help converts understand the great truths surrounding the triunity of God, they would be more likely to stand fast when tempted to stray. A high conception of the greatness of God is one of the best antidotes to the temptations of worldliness, the attractiveness of sin, and the appealing claims of world religions and heretical sects. This high conception is clearly in view in believers' baptism "in the name of the Father and of the Son and of the Holy Spirit."

Let all things their Creator bless,
And worship him in humbleness,
Hallelujah! Hallelujah!
Praise, praise the Father, praise the Son,
And praise the Spirit, Three in One.
(Francis of Assisi 1182 - 1226)

9.
The Trinity and our resources

Conversion, baptism and union with the Lord's people in a local church are but the beginning of a life of faith, and the very essence of this life is growth. This is evident from the way the Bible describes the Christian life. For example, we become children of God (1 John 3:1) and disciples of Jesus Christ (Acts 6:1). Both childhood and discipleship imply growth in spiritual strength and understanding. In this chapter we will explore the relationship between the three persons of the Holy Trinity and this necessary spiritual progress.

We can see such progress illustrated in the account of the creation of the world (Genesis 1). The Bible teaches us that all three persons were involved in that momentous display of God's glory (Genesis 1:1-3; Psalm 33: 6-9; and Colossians 1:16-17). The initial act of bringing into being something out of nothing was followed by development and growth. Gradually, the whole world was teeming with life and adorned with colour. All this was preparing the way for the crown of God's handiwork — humankind. This is a picture of the Christian life and its development, as Paul wrote " ... if anyone is in Christ, he is a new creation" (2 Corinthians 5:17). Just as the Father, Son and Holy Spirit were together in the creation of the world, so each of them is involved in our spiritual creation and growth in spiritual strength and vitality.

The benediction

We often end a service of worship with the benediction:

> May the grace of the Lord Jesus Christ, and the love of God, and the fellowship of the Holy Spirit be with you all (2 Corinthians 13:14).

Honesty compels us to admit that all too frequently the reciting of those words is a mere formal "signing off". Worse still, it signals the time to turn our minds to other things. This is very sad, because here is a pronouncement of considerable importance for our ongoing spiritual life. During the service we may well have been reminded of the demands of growth in the Christian life, perhaps in terms of holy living, Christian service, or boldness in our witness to Jesus Christ. If we have taken the message seriously, we will have a sense of challenge and a feeling of inadequacy for the task. This benediction should come to us as a tremendous boost to our resolve and an encouragement to respond positively to the message. It is an assurance of the spiritual resources available to us in our triune God. That being so, let us examine it in a little more detail.

The grace of our Lord Jesus Christ — This is often explained in terms of salvation blessing, the love of Christ for undeserving sinners, which is certainly included. But as we have said, the benediction is a reminder of our resources in the triune God for living out the Christian life. Here, then, the grace of Christ is the strengthening he gives, as Paul himself experienced it. Earlier in the same letter, Paul tells how he begged the Lord to take away what he calls his "thorn in the flesh":

> But he said to me, "My grace is sufficient for you, for my power is made perfect in weakness." Therefore I will boast all the more gladly about my weaknesses, so that Christ's power may rest on me (2 Corinthians 12:9).

Because of this, the same apostle was able to say:

> I can do everything through him who gives me strength
> (Philippians 4:13).

We must also notice that in the benediction Paul lists several titles of our Lord. The complete list is used by Peter:

> But grow in the grace and knowledge of our Lord and Saviour
> Jesus Christ (2 Peter 3:18).

Lord — this is the divine name: all that we learn about God in the Old Testament can be poured into it. His resources at our disposal are the inexhaustible riches of the love, wisdom and power of God.

Saviour — he is the one Peter called "our God and Saviour Jesus Christ" (2 Peter 1:1) and who gave himself for us so that through his death our sins might be forgiven. Will he who suffered unspeakable agony for us deny us the whole scope of his resources?

Jesus — the Son became man and he is able to help us, not only because he is God, but also because he knows from experience our needs and how we feel (Hebrews 2:16-18 and 4:14-16). God and man! What a combination!

Christ — he is the one promised from Old Testament days and anointed to be to us a prophet to give us wisdom, a priest to give us access to the Father and a king to provide all our needs and to rule lovingly over us.

It is no wonder that Paul is able to write:

> my God will meet all your needs according to his glorious riches in Christ Jesus (Philippians 4:19).

The love of God — we may wonder why the order of the three persons is different in this benediction from that given in Matthew 28:19, and we can only guess at the answer. One reason might be that the Corinthian church tended to lack Christlikeness in character and so needed an emphasis on the grace of Jesus Christ, so Paul mentions that first. Another reason could be that Jesus is the way of entry for us into the blessings of the Father and the Spirit. It is only as we renounce any idea of personal merit to commend us to God, and learn to trust only and completely in Jesus Christ, that we can experience the love of God and the fellowship of the Holy Spirit.

What a wonderful resource we have in the love of God. There is nothing more encouraging and stimulating than the assurance that in Jesus Christ we have entered into the heart of our heavenly Father, and that despite our shortcomings, failures and sins, his love for us does not waver.

The fellowship of the Holy Spirit — if we should begin to doubt the grace of our Lord Jesus Christ or the love of God the Father, the Holy Spirit's ministry is to make these blessings real to us. He unites us both to the Son and to the Father, and also to the Lord's people. In a profound sense the church is the fellowship of the Holy Spirit. This means that we have available to us all the benefits of the prayers, fellowship and ministries of the church — the communion of saints.

> A Christian is one who seeks and enjoys the grace of the Lord Jesus, the love of God, and the communion of the Holy Ghost. (*Commentary on 2 Corinthians,* Charles Hodge,)

It is not surprising that Dr. Campbell Morgan, a former minister at London's Westminster Chapel, should plead that in our services of worship nothing should come after such a benediction.

Such are the resources for holy living available to every Christian, and they are ours through the Lord Jesus Christ. But we are not to be entirely passive in these things. We are to use the means available to us to draw on these resources for our growth in grace. It is this personal responsibility that Jude emphasises in his New Testament letter:

> But you, dear friends, build yourselves up in your most holy faith and pray in the Holy Spirit. Keep yourselves in God's love as you wait for the mercy of our Lord Jesus Christ to bring you to eternal life (Jude 20-21).

We see that Jude, like the other New Testament writers, puts the matter in trinitarian terms.

Jude's subject at this point is the need to build ourselves up in our faith, which is another way of describing growth in the Christian life. He gives three ways in which we can do this — praying, keeping and waiting.

Pray in the Spirit — later, we will devote a whole chapter to the effect of trinitarian thinking on our prayer life (chapter twelve). Here we note the important fact that prayer is essential to our spiritual growth. We are to seek the guidance of the Holy Spirit in our prayers, and to ask for his daily "filling" (Ephesians 5:18) to enable us to make progress.

Remain in God's love — the assurance of God's love in the benediction does not take away from us the need to keep ourselves within the boundaries of that love. This involves separation from all that offends or grieves our heavenly Father. It therefore includes the diligent study of the Scriptures to be reminded of the kind of life that pleases him. Only those who are, in practice, keeping themselves in God's love can be sure that they have been embraced from eternity by that love.

Wait for the Lord's return — the Lord who gave himself for us on the cross will complete his work of mercy when he returns to take us to be with him for ever (1 Thessalonians 4:15-17). A constant theme of the New Testament is the way that anticipation of the Lord's return works toward our progress in holiness (1 Thessalonians 3:13 and 2 Peter 3:11-14).

Once again we have seen the practical value of the fact that our God is a triunity. We need to take time to work this out for ourselves in the light of these Scriptures. For instance, C.H.Spurgeon wrote that a Christian is someone who can say:

I trust in a triune God. I trust the Father, believing that he has chosen me before the foundations of the world; I trust him to provide for me in providence, to teach me, to guide me, to correct me if need be, and to bring me home to his own house where the many mansions are. I trust the Son. Very God of very God is he — the man Christ Jesus. I trust in him to take away all my sins by his own sacrifice, and to adorn me with his perfect righteousness. I trust him to be my intercessor, to present my prayers and desires before his Father's throne, and I trust him to be my advocate at the last great day, to plead my cause and to justify me. I trust him for what he is, for what he has done, and for what he has promised yet to do. And I trust the Holy Spirit — I trust him to drive out all my sins; I trust him to curb my temper, to subdue my will, to enlighten my understanding, to check my passions, to comfort my despondency, to help my weakness, to illuminate my darkness; I trust him to dwell in me as my life, to reign in me as my King, to sanctify me wholly, spirit, soul and body, and then to take me up to dwell with the saints in light for ever.

(From *Climbing the Heights* compiled by Al Bryant)

We see then that we have amazing spiritual resources in the triune God enabling us to live a life of faith. This robs us of every excuse for living weak, Christian lives. In the Trinity, surely, is the secret of spiritual strength and stability.

Laud and honour to the Father,
Laud and honour to the Son,
Laud and honour to the Spirit,
Ever Three and ever One;
One in might, and One in glory,
While unending ages run.

(7th C., tr. John M. Neale, 1818 - 66)

10.
The Trinity and assurance (1)

Over forty years ago I was the speaker at a weekend of meetings for young people. I was allowed to choose my own subject and as a consequence the young people endured four long sessions on the doctrine of the Trinity! At about the half-way point, one bold young man, after my own heart, asked, "but where does all this get us to, what is the purpose of it all?" He was beginning to feel that the subject was not very practical. Of course, it had been necessary to lay a good foundation in the doctrine before applying it to our spiritual experience, but when at last we came to the application, I felt that the most helpful thing I could do was to concentrate on the subject of this chapter — the Trinity and our assurance of salvation.

This is a very important theme. When we are sure of our salvation we are joyful Christians and strong in our faith. This, in turn, makes us more effective in our witness to unbelieving people around us. We may talk to them about what the Bible teaches, but our words are more convincing when they are backed up by a life characterised by quiet confidence.

Perhaps the best way for us to explore this is simply to refer to a number of texts with a minimum of comment, allowing them to speak for themselves. We will deal with them in their biblical sequence rather than work out a logical argument. As we do this we may be surprised by how much the Bible has to say on this subject.

John 6: 37-44

All that the Father gives me will come to me, and whoever comes to me I will never drive away … No-one can come to me unless the Father who sent me draws him, and I will raise him up at the last day.

Any idea that election is something we find only in Paul's writings is contradicted by this and other passages in the gospels (e.g. John 17:2,6,9 and 24). The point here is the absolute agreement between the choice of the Father and the work of the Holy Spirit in drawing the chosen ones to love and to trust Jesus Christ. This is even clearer when we observe that the drawing involved is said to be by the Father — it is impossible for him to contradict himself. No-one should hesitate to embrace Jesus Christ because of uncertainty as to whether the Father has chosen them. Those who come to Christ are elect! Furthermore, the harmony of the work of the three persons is assuring to us because those who are led by the Spirit to trust in Christ cannot be lost. The Son and the Father are agreed about this and the Son will most assuredly fulfil the Father's purpose in election and "raise them up at the last day".

John 10: 27-30

My sheep listen to my voice; I know them, and they follow me. I give them eternal life, and they shall never perish; no-one can snatch them out of my hand. My Father, who has given them to me, is greater than all; no-one can snatch them out of my Father's hand. I and the Father are one.

Although the Holy Spirit is not mentioned in our first text or in these verses, his work is clearly in evidence. Jesus was surrounded by people hardened in their unbelief. There is a tremendous contrast between them and those who listen to Jesus and follow him. Only the Holy Spirit can work this miracle. Those who follow Jesus are like sheep, vulnerable to attack from wolves that want to destroy them. These "wolves" are false teachers, or anyone else who would try to destroy the faith of Christ's followers, or lead them into sin.

But Jesus and the Spirit are at one, and those in whom the Spirit has begun his work come under Christ's protection with his assurance that he will not fail any of them.

We might think that our Lord's words in this passage are enough for our comfort and peace of mind, but there is additional assurance to be found in the fact underlying the text that it is a threefold cord that secures our complete salvation (Ecclesiastes 4:12). The Father initiated the process in eternity by giving a countless number of people to the Son. Having done this, there is no way he will forget or neglect them. We are safe in the hands of both the Father and the Son. Again, we might be satisfied with such an assurance, but the Lord knows how prone we are to doubts and fears, so he adds, "I and the Father are one". At the very least this means that the Father and the Son are united in their determination to protect and preserve all those whom the Spirit has led to submit to Jesus Christ for salvation from sin and its consequences. But there is yet more here for our consolation. Jesus meant, not only that he and the Father are of one mind, but also that he and the Father are one being. This leads us to the amazing truth that if it were possible for anyone to be dropped or wrenched from the protecting care of the Son and the Father, then there would be a schism in the very being of God himself! The full implication of our Lord's words here is that if any true believer in Christ could be lost for ever, then God would no longer be God.

Romans 8: 1-3
Therefore, there is now no condemnation for those who are in Christ Jesus, because through Christ Jesus the law of the Spirit of life set me free from the law of sin and death. For what the law was powerless to do in that it was weakened by the sinful nature, God did by sending his own Son in the likeness of sinful man to be a sin offering.

Like so much of Paul's writings, these verses contain a very condensed and closely reasoned argument; they are not easy to grasp without detailed study. However, we can extract some facts from them showing how the truth of the Trinity helps us to be assured of our salvation.

Paul tells us that certain people are no longer condemned. The Father is the judge of all (Genesis 18:25; Matthew 10:28,32-33; Hebrews 10:30-31) and left to ourselves we are all under his judgement and subject to his wrath (Romans 1:18). But for these people the judgement has been set aside and God's wrath has been appeased. The question arises as to the identity of these people who receive such mercy. How can we be sure that we are no longer under condemnation? The answer is by taking note of the work of the Son and the Holy Spirit.

First, the Son, Jesus Christ, has set us free from the demands of God's law. That law condemns us because we break it; we fail to obey its requirements. But Jesus has suffered the punishment due to us and his total obedience is credited to us. Because of this, those who trust in Jesus Christ are no longer condemned.

When we are tempted to doubt our salvation we should look again to Jesus Christ and refresh our minds with what he has done for us. But there is something more. There is the work of the Holy Spirit within us, and this assurance of "no condemnation" is for those who "do not live according to the sinful nature but according to the Spirit". The Spirit has enabled them to turn from trusting in themselves and to trust in God's mercy through Jesus Christ. He has given them a desire to live in a way that pleases God and be useful in spreading the gospel. Then, so that our doubts will be completely subdued, we learn that it was the Father, who rightly condemned us, who himself sent his Son into the world to die for us. So here again we see the threefold cord of Father, Son and Holy Spirit making our salvation secure.

Romans 8: 29-30
For those God foreknew he also predestined to be conformed to the likeness of his Son, that he might be the firstborn among many brothers. And those he predestined, he also called; those he called, he also justified; those he justified, he also glorified.

This is probably the best known passage of Scripture laying down the ground of our assurance in the integrated work of Father, Son and Holy Spirit. Paul reminds us that our salvation began with God in what we may call, for want of better language, eternity past. He foreknew and predestined us to be saved. This is not something to be understood but to be gratefully received.

We should take note that all three aspects of our salvation are included here. First there is the liberation from the power of sin beginning the process of conforming us "to the likeness of his Son". Then there is justification which means that we are delivered from the penalty of sin and reconciled to God who declares us to be righteous. Finally we will be glorified — ultimately freed from every trace of the presence of sin in us as well as in the whole of creation.

The great thing about this passage is the way Paul ties everything together so tightly — predestined, therefore called, therefore justified, therefore glorified. Or, to put that another way, chosen by the Father, therefore called by the Spirit, therefore justified through Jesus Christ.

We will continue this theme in the next chapter, and there work out some important conclusions to be drawn for our assurance from the mass of evidence we have in the Bible. Meanwhile let us simply observe that the Bible clearly intends us to draw confidence, not only from the involvement of the three persons of the Trinity in our salvation, but also from their unity in love and purpose. If it were possible for anyone to slip out of that love and purpose, having once been embraced by it, then there would be a catastrophic fissure in the very being of God. Since this is impossible, let those who trust in Jesus Christ for pardon and reconciliation to God be assured that they are secure.

But let us all examine ourselves to be sure that we are among those who follow Jesus Christ as sheep follow a shepherd, and who have a sincere desire to please God and to be transformed into perfection like our Lord himself.

Take heart and trust in God
the Father and the Son —
God is our strength and shield,
His Spirit guides us on:

Let trumpets sound and people sing,
The Lord through all the earth is King.
                              (David Mowbray)

11.
The Trinity and assurance (2)

The Lord intends that believers should be strong in faith and in assurance. This is clear from the many ways in which the Bible seeks to give us confidence that those who trust in Jesus Christ are secure for eternity. In this chapter we will glance briefly at three more texts and then consider some of the conclusions we can draw.

Galatians 4: 4-6

When the time had fully come, God sent his Son, born of a woman, born under law, to redeem those under law, that we might receive the full rights of sons. Because you are sons, God sent the Spirit of his Son into our hearts, the Spirit who calls out, "Abba, Father".

The picture here is of children, having been under the care and training of guardians, who have now reached the age when they are released from those teachers, and enter into the full privileges of children.

We are all born "under law" (the guardian) by which we are condemned (Galatians 3:10), but God has sent his Son into the world and through his death we are released from that situation. The result is that we are able to enjoy all the privileges of being "sons of God" including anticipation of a glorious inheritance.

The additional help to our assurance here is that the same Father who sent his Son to save us, also sends his Spirit into our hearts to assure us, giving us the warrant to feel at liberty and to enter into fellowship with the Father. Again we see the three persons of the

Trinity acting in perfect harmony to change sinful human beings into beloved children of God.

Ephesians 1:3-7, and 13-14.

Praise be to the God and Father of our Lord Jesus Christ, ... For he chose us in him before the creation of the world to be holy and blameless in his sight ... In him we have redemption through his blood, the forgiveness of sins, in accordance with the riches of God's grace ... Having believed, you were marked in him with a seal, the promised Holy Spirit, who is a deposit guaranteeing our inheritance.

These verses spell out once more the trinitarian nature of our salvation.The Father chooses, the Son redeems, the Holy Spirit seals. There are two new elements for us to take to heart. The first is the union of the Father and the Son in choosing those who would be saved. Other Scriptures have taught us that it is the Father who chooses his people, loves them and marks them out as his own. But here we are told that "he chose us in him (Jesus Christ)" which means in union with Jesus Christ. We deduce from this that our salvation is rooted in perfect agreement between the Father and the Son in eternity past, that those whom the Father chose would most certainly be redeemed by the Son.

The second element here for us to notice is that the Father seals those who trust in Christ with the Holy Spirit. He is like a seal on a document or a piece of property indicating ownership and protection. The Spirit is the Father's mark of possession and therefore of security. The Spirit is not only, as we have seen (Galatians 4:4-6), the one who enables us to call God Father, but is himself the guarantee of our security.

Titus 3: 4-6.

When the kindness and love of God our Saviour appeared, he saved us, not because of righteous things we had done, but because of his mercy. He saved us through the washing of rebirth and renewal by the Holy Spirit, whom he poured out on us generously through Jesus Christ our Saviour.

This is the last of the trinitarian passages we will consider, that help us toward assurance of our salvation. Here we see that those whom Jesus Christ came to save are also renewed by the Holy Spirit, who is sent by the Father because of all that Jesus Christ has done for them. An interesting point in this passage is the close identity of the Father with the Son. Notice how Paul puts it, "when the kindness and love of God our Saviour appeared". He says almost the same thing in the previous chapter (2:10-11). By this we understand that when Jesus Christ came into the world it was God himself who broke through into human history with kindness and love. This calls to mind the story of Abraham climbing mount Moriah with his son Isaac to offer him as a sacrifice as God commanded him (Genesis 22:1-19). Twice in that story we read the poignant words "the two of them went on together". We can almost hear the throb of the father's heart as he anticipated the awful deed from which he was ultimately spared. But God neither spared himself nor his Son from the terrible ordeal of the cross (Romans 8:32) — the two of them went together!

Having reviewed these Scriptures in the last chapter and in this one, let now draw out some reasonable deductions from what we have learned. First, it is well for us to face the fact that there is such a thing as false assurance. In other words, there are people who are sure they are Christians on the road to heaven, but whose confidence is misplaced.

Antidotes to false assurance

For many such deluded people, the trinitarian nature of salvation is the perfect antidote to their illusion. Very often, the problem is that they are relying on one person of the Trinity to the exclusion of the other two.

The Father alone — this is probably the most common cause of false assurance. Too often people declare their belief in God, but they have no place for Jesus Christ or for the Holy Spirit. Mostly, these people also think that the way to heaven is by obeying God's laws and they think that their efforts to do so will be sufficient. But this is an impossible situation, because the Father in whom they profess to believe cannot be separated from the Son whom he sent to rescue people who have broken his laws. Nor can the Father be isolated from the Spirit he gives to enable people to live in relationship with him. It is an insult to the Father to ignore his Son and his Holy Spirit. If the Father says we need the Son and the Spirit, and that without them we cannot have fellowship with him, it is sheer pride for any of us to think otherwise.

The Son without the Spirit — there are those who profess to believe in Jesus Christ as their Saviour, but whose lives are indistinguishable from people who are not Christians. Some of them think that their faith in Christ proves they are also among God's elect. When we look at this situation with trinitarian spectacles on, we can see immediately just how impossible it is. As we have seen, those whom the Father chose, the Son came to save and the Holy Spirit begins to change, and in this the three are entirely at one. There is no salvation apart from a changed life; we are to be saved both from the guilt of sin and from its power. It is a terrible delusion to think that we can be eternally secure while living carelessly and having no sincere desire to be holy.

The Spirit without the Son — this is false assurance based on the fact that one's life is changed, but there is no conscious reliance on Christ crucified for reconciliation to God. Such people have an experience that they believe is of the Holy Spirit, but they have little or no realisation that they are hell-deserving sinners under the wrath of God, needing to trust Jesus Christ as their Saviour and the one who alone can reconcile them to God. Our reflections on the Scriptures have taught us that it is only those who are reconciled to the Father by the Son who receive the Holy Spirit. We have also seen that the Holy Spirit not only changes people's lives, but also leads them to Jesus Christ. No coming to Christ means no work of the Spirit, no matter how radically our lives have been changed by other means.

The experience of such people is more likely to be psychological than spiritual. Our lives can be radically changed for better or worse, by all kinds of means, such as by turning to an eastern religion or some heretical sect, by transcendental meditation or by psychiatric treatment. But none of these is the work of the Holy Spirit. Some changes might even seem to be the work of the Holy Spirit because they have occurred within a church setting. But if we have not sought and found pardon for our sin through Jesus Christ, we are still condemned sinners.

We see, then, another way in which standing on the doctrine of the Trinity is a practical help. It is certainly an effective antidote to false assurance, but it also provides us with good arguments towards true assurance.

Arguments for true assurance

Let us track down some of the reasons why some Christians lack assurance:

I don't know if I can keep up the Christian life — this doubt often assails people who come to see their need of Jesus Christ to save them from their sin and its consequences, but do not realise how much they need him after that. Then, when they are confronted with the requirement to live godly and holy lives, they begin to doubt. This is understandable, and it is a very good thing for all of us to realise our inability to keep up Christian standards with our own resources. But the doubts and fears should be dispelled by the knowledge that the Son and the Holy Spirit are in harmony, and that there is no way that the Son will save anyone from their guilt without giving them the Holy Spirit to release them from the power of their sins. Furthermore, as we have seen, the Father and the Son are at one in their purpose that nothing in the whole universe will take those who trust in Christ away from him.

I can believe in Jesus but not the Father — this problem is on the increase, partly because of the abuse some children have received from their fathers. Their understanding of God the Father is distorted by the memory of such experiences. The answer to this is to be found in the fact of the Trinity. There is no difference between the love the Father has for us and the love of the Son and of the Spirit. The Son would not have come into the world to save us if the Father had not loved us enough to send him (John 3:16). Furthermore, the Holy Spirit puts the love of the Father into our hearts (Romans 5:5). We cannot have one person of the Trinity without the others — and that is a good thing.

I don't know if I am elect — here are people who are conscious of their sinfulness and of their need to trust in Jesus Christ as their Lord and Saviour. They long to be able to commit themselves to Christ and find in him their peace with God. But the whole question of whether they are among God's elect becomes a great hindrance to them. These dear people do not realise they are trying to do the impossible — dividing the Trinity. If only they would ask themselves how they came to have such feelings of sinfulness and desires to be right with God! The only possible answer to that question is that the Holy Spirit has brought them to those convictions. Now, since the three persons of the Trinity are in complete harmony, there is no way that the Spirit will open the eyes of people whom the Father has not chosen or for whom the Son has not died. Those who long to be saved must make bold to trust in Christ and to rejoice that they have been loved by the Father from before time.

I am too great a sinner for the Lord to save me — sometimes things like this are said in a cynical or light-hearted manner by people who are not at all concerned about their spiritual state. For them, the fact is that so long as they continue in such a frame of mind they will not be saved. But there are people, deeply concerned about their relationship with God, who hesitate to believe that God is willing to pardon such sinners as they are. Also, some people, who are already Christians, begin to doubt their salvation because of their persistent sinning. If only such people would realise that God's salvation is rooted in the great covenant between the Father, the Son and the Holy Spirit before the world began, they would not doubt the depth of God's love and his willingness to pardon the vilest of sinners and constantly to forgive those who look for his mercy.

It is tremendously important that we should enjoy a large measure of assurance to give vitality to our life and witness. There could scarcely be a stronger argument for the restoration of the Trinity to a bigger place in Christian thinking and experience.

Holy Spirit, Lord, proceeding
From the Father and the Son,
You're the seal of our salvation
Live and reign within our hearts.
Father, Son and Holy Spirit,
You alone are God Most High.
Maker, Saviour, Sanctifier,
Lord and God we praise your name!
(C.J.Laslett)

(Readers may also like to know of the book *How can I be sure?* also published by Grace Publications, ISBN 0-946462-57-7

12.
The Trinity and prayer

Prayer is probably the greatest thing that we can experience on earth. The whole idea that people like us can speak to the Creator of all things who is unspeakably holy and glorious, should fill us with astonishment.

But honesty compels most of us to admit that we rarely have this sense of thrill and amazement. We are more likely to treat prayer as a rather commonplace routine resulting at times in feelings of futility and emptiness. Even if our experience is more satisfying than this, we will still confess a need for our prayer times to be enriched to a greater degree.

One way, perhaps the best way, for this to happen is for us to realise afresh the application of the Trinity to our prayer life. You might think that to do this would make prayer more complicated and a great burden. But many of us have discovered the opposite as prayer has taken on a new sense of reality, and has increased in breadth and depth. The key text on this subject is in Paul's letter to the Ephesians:

> For through him (Jesus) we both (Jews and Gentiles) have access to the Father by one Spirit (Ephesians 2:18).

Commenting on this verse, Dr.D.M.Lloyd-Jones said:

> Here, in this statement, the Apostle reaches his grand climax. There is nothing beyond this, this is the very top, the acme. This is the very quintessence of the Christian faith and the Christian position. There is no doubt, therefore, that

we are looking at and considering one of the mightiest and most glorious statements that is to be found in the whole range of Scripture ... Our chief trouble is that we do not realise the meaning of things like this. Were we to do so the Christian church would be revolutionised.

This text immediately presents us with a basic order for prayer. The Father is the one to whom we pray and we approach him through Jesus Christ with the help of the Holy Spirit.This order is not intended for us to follow slavishly; it does not undermine our liberty. But we are reminded of what makes prayer possible and it is good for us to have it constantly in mind.

Our Father

Prayer is primarily to be directed to God the Father because he is:

the official representative of all three divine persons in their joint-dealings with us. He acts on behalf of the whole Trinity, so that in our relationship with him as our Father we are actually relating to the Son and the Spirit too. This role of representative belongs naturally to the Father because he is the first person of the Trinity ... It isn't that you should worship him to the exclusion of the Lord Jesus Christ and the Holy Spirit. Of course not. What I mean is this: when you worship the whole Trinity as one God, without distinguishing the persons, then you should direct your worship specifically to the Father.

(*What happens when I pray?*, Dr.N.R.Needham,)

Jesus himself taught his disciples "Our Father in heaven, hallowed be your name" (Matthew 6:9) and also, when he himself prayed, "Father, the time has come" (John 17:1). This takes us into a breadth of prayer for us to explore. We can range from exultant adoration of the greatness and majesty of God to the enjoyment of our Father's love and care. These two aspects of prayer are all too often allowed to exclude each other. We have either feelings of awe and reverence, or a sense of loving liberty — but not together at one and the same time. This is a pity because it unnecessarily limits our prayers and robs us of their full orbed blessings. The hymn writer puts words into our mouths:

> O how I fear thee, living God
> With deepest, tenderest fears,
> And worship Thee with trembling hope
> And penitential tears!
>
> Yet I may love Thee, too, O Lord,
> Almighty as Thou art,
> For Thou hast stooped to ask of me
> The love of my poor heart.
> (Frederick W. Faber 1814 - 63)

Access through Jesus Christ

Nothing must be allowed to blot out from our memories the contrast between the holiness of God "who lives in unapproachable light", and our sinfulness and unworthiness to enter his presence. The question arises:

> O how shall I, whose native sphere
> Is dark, whose mind is dim,
> Before the ineffable appear,
> And on my naked spirit bear
> The uncreated beam?
> (Thomas Binney 1798-1874)

The answer to the agonising question posed in that verse is "through him (Jesus Christ) we both have access by one Spirit to the Father". There is a wonderful trinitarian dimension to our prayers, and we learn here first of all that our right to enter God's presence is in his

Son. This is both through what he has done for us and through what he is.

Our sinful state has put up a barrier between us and God. This barrier is impassable except through Jesus Christ:

> For there is one God and one mediator between God and men, the man Christ Jesus (1 Timothy 2:5).

It was necessary for two things to happen. Our guilt needed to be removed and our sinful pollution dealt with. Jesus Christ has answered both of these requirements. He took our guilt to himself and suffered its penalty, thus removing it, and opening the way of prayer:

> Let us then approach the throne of grace with confidence (Hebrews 4:16).

A holy God is nauseated by our sin, but we will not be entirely rid of it this side of heaven. Jesus Christ, God's Son, deals with this pollution by covering it with his own sinlessness, making us acceptable to the Father. He is the only means available to us of access into the Father's presence.

Recently I was standing at the door of the former home of the playwright G.B.Shaw — now a tourist attraction. It was outside visiting time and I had no right of entry, not even at a price, as was obvious on the face of the curator! "But", I said "I know I have no right to come in, but my sister is here and when Mr. Shaw was alive she worked for him!" Immediately the door opened wide to my sister. I assumed I would be left standing. But no! "You can come in too!" I had access, but only on the basis of my sister's merit. So it is that we have access into God's presence through our Lord's merits. This should give us a tremendous sense of privilege and greatly excite our love and gratitude.

There may be times when we feel that our prayer life is a failure and our worship altogether inadequate. Here again, the mediation of Christ is the answer for our comfort. He offers to God his own perfection for our acceptance, and this of necessity includes the worship we owe to God. This is no excuse for us to become careless in our devotions, but it does relieve us of a sense of guilt and give us even more reason to praise Jesus Christ for all he does for us.

A big question mark

This puts a very big question mark over any and every attempt to pray to God without relying on the mediation of Jesus Christ. There are those who practise transcendental meditation and other forms of mental exercise in the belief that they are finding God by such methods. They are surely mistaken, because they are guilty of putting their wisdom against God's wisdom. He tells us that we need a mediator, but they presume to know better. He sent his only Son to be the mediator, but they choose to ignore him. We all need to acknowledge that our sin makes us unacceptable to God apart from Jesus Christ, and to delight in the certainty that we do have access through him.

By the Spirit

Our God is very wise and gracious. He knows that we have problems that would hinder us from enjoying the full potential of the privilege of prayer. So he helps us to overcome those problems by ministering to us by the Holy Spirit.

The desire to pray

Left to ourselves we would not pray, but the Holy Spirit's work is to bring to fulfilment all that the Father and the Son make possible. His aim is always to direct us both to the Father and the Son. He creates in us a desire to pray to the Father and to enjoy fellowship with him:

... those who are led by the Spirit of God are sons of God. For you did not receive a spirit that makes you a slave again to fear, but you received the Spirit of sonship. And by him we cry, 'Abba, Father' (Romans 8: 14-15).

The Spirit also leads us to rely on Jesus Christ as the mediator through whom we are welcomed by the Father.

How to pray

For many Christians the difficulty is not the desire to pray, but how to do so. They have a great affinity with the twelve disciples of Jesus when they came to him with the request "Lord, teach us to pray, just as John taught his disciples" (Luke 11:1). There must have been something about our Lord's attitude when he prayed. Perhaps it was a sensitive balance between reverence and liberty that we mentioned earlier. Perhaps the disciples marvelled at our Lord's concentration in prayer or at the ease with which he turned to the Father spontaneously when occasion arose. In such matters, the Holy Spirit is our helper.

What to pray for

In the same way, the Spirit helps us in our weakness. We do not know what we ought to pray for, but the Spirit himself intercedes for us with groans that words cannot express (Romans 8:26).

Most of us pray about too few things and we need this ministry of the Holy Spirit to prompt us about the scope of prayer open to us. He does this in a number of ways. One is to show us the teaching in the Bible about prayer, and especially the examples we find there. A consideration of the prayer Jesus taught his disciples will help

(Matthew 6:9-13), as also will a perusal of such prayers as those of Daniel (Daniel 9:4-19), or Paul (Ephesians 3:14-19; Colossians 1: 9-14). The Spirit also reminds us that there are different kinds of prayer as Paul indicated —

> And pray in the Spirit on all occasion with all kinds of prayers and requests (Ephesians 6:18).

If we are led by the Spirit, our prayers will include adoration, praise, thanksgiving, confession, repentance, love, intercession and requests.

In addition to directing us to Scripture, the Holy Spirit also inclines our hearts and minds to pray for certain things. Perhaps we hear a sermon that exposes a needy area in our lives, or a missionary speaker tells of people in difficult situations, and we feel a burden to pray about these things. It is in such ways that the Spirit stimulates our prayers, and we must be sensitive to him and responsive to his touch. Here then is Thomas Binney's answer to his own question quoted above (page 94):

> There is a way for man to rise
> To that sublime abode;
> An offering and a sacrifice,
> A Holy Spirit's energies,
> An Advocate with God.

A Basic Order

The question arises as to whether the order — through the Son, by the Spirit, to the Father — must be rigidly adhered to. May we not also pray to the Son or to the Holy Spirit? The answer is that this order is basic but not exclusive. A very imperfect illustration could be learning to drive a car. The instructor will instil into our minds a basic procedure for making the stationary car move away from the road side: make sure the road is clear, signal your intention, then move off. With experience, we will not usually stray from that order, but even so, there may be occasions when we think it right to vary the procedure and no-one will condemn us for doing so, unless we cause an accident.

Not many Christians will deny that we are at liberty to pray to Jesus Christ, God's Son. We have examples of this in the New Testament (Matthew 15:25; Luke 23: 42; and Acts 7: 59), and, since the Son is God, we have no inhibitions about worshipping him with thanksgiving and seeking his help.

However, many believers will not pray to the Holy Spirit. This is mainly for two reasons. One reason is that there is no example of prayer to the Holy Spirit in Scripture. Another is that the Holy Spirit points to the Father and to the Son, and does not draw attention to himself. These are weighty considerations, and I respect them, but the equality of the three persons of the Trinity in one God seems to me to give us a warrant at least to thank the Spirit for his gracious ministry and to seek his help as we work out our lives as Christians.

There is one other practical matter to mention. The order set out in Ephesians 2:18 leads some earnest Christians to believe that they must refer to it every time they pray in private or in public. This seems to be unnecessary; the Lord knows our hearts and the honour we would pay to all three persons of the Trinity. This question arises especially in public prayer meetings where each person feels it necessary to remind the Lord that the right approach is being made. Is it not enough for the leader of the meeting, or the first person to pray, to lay down the ground of approach to God, leaving the rest to feel at liberty to build on that foundation?

We began by suggesting that a trinitarian understanding of prayer would give it new breadth and make it more exhilarating. This certainly will be the experience of those who take it seriously.

Jehovah! Father, Spirit, Son!
Mysterious Godhead! Three in One!
Before Thy throne we sinners bend:
Grace, pardon, life to us extend.
(Edward Cooper 1770-1833)

13.
The Trinity and Communion with God

Many a parent knows how remarkably phone bills will become more expensive when a son has acquired a girl friend or a daughter has taken the eye of a young man. A courting couple who live many miles apart will value every letter they receive from each other and every phone call, no matter how short. This is all exciting and helpful, but it is not nearly so satisfying and fulfilling as living together in marriage.

Prayer can be likened to the phone calls (or e-mail, if you're into that), while communion is more like living together as husband and wife. We may properly think of the Christian life as living together with God, like Enoch, of whom it is said he "walked with God" (Genesis 5:22). But this can become rather vague and indefinite if it is not focused in times of communion with God in which we meditate on him. This is at the heart of the blessing of eternal life which is ours in Jesus Christ. Our Lord defined this in his prayer:

> Now this is eternal life; that they may know you, the only
> true God, and Jesus Christ, whom you have sent (John 17:3).

The knowledge here is a close relationship of love, reminding us that eternal life is not only everlasting, but is a life of fellowship, or communion with God. Our Lord's words also introduce us to the trinitarian nature of this communion, in which we experience, in a positive manner, a love relationship with both the Father and the Son. We will explore this in a little more detail, but first, let us notice in passing some confirmations of what we have said so far. For example, we have our Lord's reply to Judas (not Judas the betrayer):

... if anyone loves me, he will obey my teaching. My Father will love him, and we will come to him and make our home with him (John 14:23).

Bishop J.C.Ryle says of this text:

These words can only admit of one sense — a spiritual and invisible coming and abiding. The Father and the Son will come spiritually into the heart and soul of a true saint, and will make their continual dwelling with him. This, again, is a purely experimental truth, and one that none can know but he that has felt it.

William Hendriksen is also helpful:

The clause, "and make our home with him", indicates a very close and intimate relationship. Father and Son, in and through the Spirit, are ever by the side of those who love their Lord, ready to comfort, ready to cheer, ready to extend all necessary help.

A home is where people live together as a family and enjoy each other's company. It is not necessary always to be chattering; more often there is silent appreciation of one another. But then there are times of sharing thoughts and common interests. This illustrates the way in which we can appreciate the Father and the Son all the time, and then enjoy times of fellowship or communion with them, distinctly and together.

The apostle John commended this trinitarian fellowship to his readers in his first letter:

We proclaim to you what we have seen and heard, so that you also may have fellowship with us. And our fellowship is with the Father and with his Son, Jesus Christ (1 John 1:3).

The absence of a mention of the Holy Spirit from these references does not diminish the trinitarian nature of this experience, because it is the Spirit who makes the experience real to us. Without doubt he also resides within us, as Paul made clear:

Do you not know that your body is a temple of the Holy
Spirit, who is in you, whom you have received from God?
(1 Corinthians 6:19)

Communion with the three persons of the Trinity is a reality for
Christians of all ages and backgrounds. For instance, consider this
example from a 17th century Puritan:

O Father, thou hast loved me and sent Jesus to redeem me;
O Jesus, thou hast loved me and assumed my nature,
    shed thine own blood to wash away my sins,
    wrought righteousness to cover my unworthiness;
O Holy Spirit, thou hast loved me and entered my heart,
    implanted there eternal life,
    revealed to me the glories of Jesus.
Three Persons and one God, I bless and praise thee,
    for love so unmerited, so unspeakable and so wondrous.
                    (*The Valley of Vision*, Banner of Truth)

In this century, a Chinese Christian has described trinitarian communion:

Love, in the heart of God, is the source of all spiritual blessing; grace expressed in Jesus Christ has made that blessing
available to us; and communion, the coming alongside of
the Holy Spirit, is the means whereby it becomes ours. What
the Father's heart devised concerning us the Son has accom-
plished for us, and now the Holy Spirit communicates it to us.
                    (*A Table in the Wilderness*, Watchman Nee)

And then a modern British theologian gives us his thoughts:

Sound spirituality needs to be thoroughly trinitarian.Neglect
the Son, lose your focus on his mediation and blood atonement and heavenly intercession, and you slip back into the
legalism that is fallen man's natural religion, the treadmill
religion of works. Again, neglect the Spirit, lose your focus
on the fellowship with Christ that he creates, the renewing of

nature that he effects, the assurance and joy he evokes, and the enabling for service that he bestows, and you slip back into orthodoxism and formalism, the religion of aspiration and perspiration without either inspiration or transformation ... Finally, neglect the Father, lose your focus on the tasks he prescribes and the discipline he inflicts, and you become a mushy, soft-centred, self-indulgent, unsteady, lazy, spoiled child in the divine family ...

(Through the Year with J.I.Packer).

The great Puritan teacher, John Owen, wrote about this communion in a very long piece entitled "Of communion with God the Father, Son, and Holy Ghost, each person distinctly in love, grace and consolation." Owen summed up his argument:

Now, of the things which have been delivered this is the sum — there is no grace whereby our souls go forth unto God, no act of divine worship yielded to him, no duty or obedience performed, but they are distinctly directed unto Father, Son, and Spirit. Now, by these and such like ways as these, do we hold communion with God; and therefore we have that communion distinctly as hath been described.

(John Owen's works Vol.2, chapter 2)

What follows here are gleanings from this work.

Communion with the Father

The substance of this communion is mutual expressions of love. The same could be said of fellowship with the Son and with the Holy Spirit, but there are Scriptures that point specifically to a love relationship with the Father. The Father's love for us is ministered to us by the Holy Spirit:

... God has poured out his love into our hearts by the Holy Spirit, whom he has given us (Romans 5:5).

This love is expressed in the most endearing and remarkable terms:

> The Lord your God is with you, he is mighty to save. He
> will take great delight in you, he will quiet you with his
> love, he will rejoice over you with singing (Zephaniah 3:17).

Communion is a two-way experience and involves our response to
the Father's assurances of love and his caring concern for us. King
David put his response into words:

> I love you, O LORD, my strength (Psalm 18:1).
> I love the LORD, for he heard my voice (Psalm 116:1).

Communion with the Son

Without doubt we are also to have a love relationship with the Son
as with the Father. Paul wrote of "the Son of God, who loved me
and gave himself for me" (Galatians 2:20). This love continues un-
broken:

> For I am convinced that neither death nor life, neither angels
> nor demons, neither the present nor the future, nor any pow-
> ers, neither height nor depth, nor anything else in all creation,
> will be able to separate us from the love of God that is in
> Christ Jesus our Lord (Romans 8:38-39).

Paul assures us that part of the blessing into which we enter when
we are converted is fellowship with Jesus Christ our Lord (1 Corinthians
1:9). The heart of this fellowship is illustrated in what we call the
communion service or Lord's Supper, where we share together with
Christ in meditation on the virtue and value of his sacrifice for us:

> Is not the cup of thanksgiving for which we give thanks a
> participation in the blood of Christ? And is not the bread
> that we break a participation in the body of Christ
> (1 Corinthians 10:16)?

But this communion is not to be confined to the occasions when we meet with others at the Lord's table. It is to be an ongoing fellowship in which we share with our Lord satisfaction in the perfection and total sufficiency of his atoning sacrifice.

Communion with the Holy Spirit

The absence of an example in Scripture of prayer to the Holy Spirit is compensated by the words of the benediction "and the fellowship of the Holy Spirit" (2 Corinthians 13:14). There is no doubt that this fellowship includes speaking to the Holy Spirit as we pray.[1] Communion with the Holy Spirit will have at least two elements. One element is thanksgiving from us for the Spirit's gracious ministry to us in changing our lives, and at the same time receiving his assurance of our salvation:

> The Spirit himself testifies with our spirit that we are God's children (Romans 8:16).

Another element in our communion with the Holy Spirit is precisely at the point of his leading us to the Father and the Son (John 15:26 and Romans 5:5). There is every good reason why we should ask the Spirit to fulfil this ministry in us and to make us fit and ready for fellowship with the Father and the Son.

We see then that scope for fellowship with God in three persons is rich and broad. It rebukes the poverty of our spiritual experience.

Perhaps this chapter can be likened to a holiday advertising brochure! A brochure opens up for us the possibility of exploring a country we know little about, and whets our appetite for the experience. Alas, sometimes the reality of the actual country is less appealing than the glowing description of it in the holiday advertisement. Communion with the Father, Son and Holy Spirit is a world to discover; and, in this case, the reality will surely exceed our expectations.

Almighty Lord, we bless Thee!
Eternal Father, Son,
And Holy, Holy Spirit —
Mysterious Three in One!
Thou hast done mighty marvels
Before our wondering gaze:
We've learnt that Thou art faithful,
In all Thy words and ways!

(W. Pennefather 1816-73)

---

[1] John Owen deals with this in the book referred to earlier and it has been simplified in the Grace Publications "Great Christian Classics" series under the title *Living with the Living God*, ISBN 0-946462-53-4

14.
The Trinity and worship

Our understanding of God is very defective if it does not result in joyful worship. The Psalmist, who as yet could not have a full view of the triune nature of God, constantly turned what he knew about God and his greatness into expressions of praise and adoration. For example:

> Sing to the LORD a new song;
>> sing to the LORD, all the earth.
> Sing to the LORD, praise his name;
>> proclaim his salvation day after day.
> Declare his glory among the nations,
>> his marvellous deeds among all peoples.
> For great is the LORD and most worthy of praise;
>> he is to be feared above all gods.
> For all the gods of the nations are idols,
>> but the LORD made the heavens (Psalm 96: 1-5).

It is very interesting that one of the early statements of the doctrine of the Trinity, known as the Athanasian creed (late 4th or early5th century AD), does not simply state that we believe this doctrine, or that this is the truth about God as we understand it, but bows in reverence with the words:

> ... the Catholic (Universal) Faith is this; That we worship one God in Trinity and Trinity in Unity ... Every encounter we have with God must lead to praise and adoration.

Different styles of worship

In churches today there are many very different forms of worship, and to a large extent these different styles reflect considerable variety in our understanding of the God we worship. For example, some churches seem to have no idea that God is a Trinity. James B. Torrance tells us that:

> Bishop Lesslie Newbigin has commented that when the average Christian in this country hears the name of God, he or she does not think of the Trinity. After many years of missionary work in India among Eastern religions, he returned to find that much worship in the west is in practice, if not in theory, unitarian.
>
> (*Worship, Community, and the Triune God of Grace*,
> Paternoster Press)

More commonly the differences in style of worship arise in part, perhaps a large part, from emphasis on one person of the Trinity with lesser stress on the others. For example, it would not be difficult for an unscrupulous preacher to work out how to earn a flattering response by suiting his approach to the atmosphere of different churches. Dwelling on the Holy Spirit in some places would secure hallelujahs; stressing in other places the love of Christ in giving himself for us would elicit some responses like, "Yes Lord", or, "Thank you, Jesus"; while two or three references to the sovereignty of God would bring forth some evangelical "grunts" in others. This, of course, is an exaggeration, but it is near enough to the truth to be uncomfortable. The atmosphere in worship in different churches varies from the sensational to the sentimental, and from the sloppy to the sombre.

You may wish to argue that this is a good thing because we all have different temperaments and preferences. If there is a variety of churches to choose from, we are more likely to find one where we can worship without hindrance or misgiving. This argument sounds reasonable and there may be some truth in it, but it is not the whole truth.

Idolatry and misrepresentation

Insofar as variations in our styles of worship reflect an emphasis on one or other of the three persons of the Trinity, we may be seriously guilty of idolatry. The God we are worshipping then is not the triune God who has made himself known to us in the Scripture. This means that we are misrepresenting God among ourselves and to the people around us. It is only the triune God who can satisfy their needs, and we are in danger of denying them that knowledge. All this is a significant part of the confusion among evangelical churches at the present time, and we need to apply ourselves prayerfully and thoughtfully to our situation.

Worship should be worthy of the God who is the object of our praise and of our submission to him as Lord. It is not something to be entered into without thought, nor should it be merely what we feel like doing at the time. We should not worship in a certain way simply because our kind of church has always done it like that. Much less should what we do be shaped by some leaders urging us to share their own style of enthusiasm in worship. There is nothing wrong with worship/song leaders as such, so long as what they do is at one with the ministry of the Word, and is not seen as something disconnected from the preaching. Worship is not a part of the service, it is the service! There is nothing wrong with enthusiasm, so long as we ask ourselves if the end product is merely human excitement or the realised presence of God.

Worship with understanding

When Paul was correcting the unbalanced situation in Corinth he wrote:

> ... I will pray with my spirit, but I will also pray with my mind; I will sing with my spirit, but I will also sing with my mind (1 Corinthians 14:15).

There are people who say that they have no use for their minds when they give themselves to the worship of God. They believe that they should be motivated by their emotions and that what they do should be spontaneous. God forbid that there should be no emotion or spontaneity in our worship, but Paul's words require us to engage our minds. We must think seriously about the one we are worshipping and then consider how what we do will be acceptable to him and bring him glory.

> Whenever we pray, whenever we come together to worship, we are worshipping this triune God. We cannot conceive of the glory and of the majesty and of the greatness, but we must try to do so. We must prepare our spirits, we must meditate, we must ponder this matter, we must search the Scriptures for it, we must see it, and having recognised it, like all men who have come near to God of whom we read in the Scriptures we shall take off our shoes from our feet, we shall feel we are men of unclean lips, we shall be conscious of the Ineffable Glory.
>
> (Dr.D.M.Lloyd-Jones on Ephesians 2:18)

But it may be that here our problem is most acute. How can we so worship that we give equal honour to the Father, the Son and the Holy Spirit, and yet be seen to worship one God?

One solution that seems to be gaining popularity, is to have different styles of worship to suit different age groups. Older people are assumed to prefer something that is very staid and largely unemotional, while young people must have something more lively and exciting. This kind of thing is to be avoided because it arises from the perceived needs of the congregation instead of from the nature and character of the God we are supposed to be worshipping. Older people need to know times of Spirit-filled exuberance, while young people must learn how to humble themselves in sober submission before a God who is holy and sovereign.

Likewise, we must not think of change in terms of what will attract "outsiders". All kinds of things unworthy of the Lord result from such an approach. But neither should we be so set in our ways that we take no account at all of the effect of what we do on people we long to see converted.

Our great concern in everything should be to follow the Scriptures as closely as we can. Since there are no set patterns of worship prescribed in the Bible we can exercise considerable liberty. However, this liberty is not to be empty-headed, but guided by the principles of Scripture and the broad spread of the examples of worship we find there.

A broad scope

It is very much easier to be dissatisfied and even critical of the present situation generally, than it is to offer suggestions that might lead to greater recognition of the triunity of our God. Perhaps our need is for all of us to explore the broad scope of worship that opens up to us if we aim at giving honour to the three persons, Father, Son and Holy Spirit. Sameness of atmosphere at all times, and in all circumstances within the life of the church, cannot possibly reflect the wide variety of expressions of worship in the Scriptures. Too often we have the same speed and the same volume of singing, whatever level that is, no matter what the subject. Consider these examples from Scripture:

Awe and wonder —

> But the LORD is in his holy temple; let all the earth be silent before him (Habakkuk 2:20).

Love and thanksgiving —

> I love the LORD, for he heard my voice; he heard my cry for mercy. Because he turned his ear to me, I will call on him as long as I live (Psalm 116:1-2).

Heart searching —

> Search me, O God, and know my heart; test
> me and know my anxious thoughts. See if there
> is any offensive way in me, and lead me in the
> way everlasting (Psalm 139: 23-24).

Confession —

> Have mercy on me, O God, according to your
> unfailing love; according to your great com-
> passion blot out my transgressions ... For I
> know my transgressions, and my sin is always
> before me. Against you, you only, have I
> sinned ... (Psalm 51:1-4).

Excitement and exuberance —

> Shout with joy to God, all the earth! Sing to the
> glory of his name; offer him glory and praise!
> Say to God, "How awesome are your deeds!"
> (Psalm 66: 1-3).

These Scriptures show something of the scope there is for variety in styles of worship. They also illustrate that the various expressions do not necessarily exclude each other. For instance, a sense of awe does not exclude excitement, and can certainly include thanksgiving.

The plea here is for a breakdown of our sameness, of whatever kind that is. There is room in one service for a variety of moods in the prayers and songs. Preparation for services can include provision for reverence in the presence of glory, sober reflection in the face of holiness, thankful love in the light of Calvary and "joy in the Holy Spirit" (Romans 14:17). This is not artificial contrivance in which there is change for no reason and a superficial aim at variety. It is genuine response to the Word of God; a thoughtful blend of spontaneity and sensitive encouragement by the way the service is led.

Almost certainly we will find it difficult to include all the possibilities for worship opened up for us when we seek to explore how to honour the Trinity in worship. It may be we should seek to spread the various emphases over a whole Sunday or even a longer period. This is a long way from attempts to "attract people" by manipulating services to please them.

We need to be humble enough to admit that our tradition, whatever it is, may not give full weight to all the Bible teaches about worship or the fullest possible glory to our triune God.

Praise ye the Father, God the Lord, who gave us,
With full and perfect love, His only Son.
Praise ye the Son who died Himself to save us;
Praise ye the Spirit, praise the Three in One!
(Margaret Cockburn-Campbell, 1808-41)

15.
The Trinity and a sense of awe

If you mention religion to some folk, they immediately associate this with a kind of mystery that only special people can penetrate. For instance, when the radio programme Classic FM has Bible readings at Easter or at other times, they hedge them around with the most eerie music to create these feelings of mystery. When a local church choir was asked to sing some new songs, their leader objected on the ground that religious music was supposed to create an atmosphere of mystery and for that reason was best sung in Latin!

We may be right to think that such notions are misguided. Nevertheless, there must be a place in Christian experience and worship for feelings of awe and wonder in the presence of majesty and mystery. But we go astray if we try to create these feelings directly. If we do that, we will probably not only resort to strange music, but also to such ideas as that God is best experienced on mountain tops, in various forms of transcendental meditation, in the tranquillity of ornate buildings, or even by the use of certain drugs. Like true peace and joy, a sense of awe is a by-product of the knowledge of God. It is not a substitute for God, nor does it necessarily lead to God.

God is knowable

Another problem with this approach is that it arises in part from the idea that God is a mystery and that, therefore, it is quite impossible for us to understand him. Indeed, if anyone dares to claim to know God, this is regarded by many people today as a delusion, or even worse, as presumption or bigotry. But God can be known in reality though not completely, and it is when we know him that 'wonder, love and praise' become a real experience. When the Queen of Sheba went to Solomon, she could say that she knew him and had talked with him. But when that relationship led to an exploration of his majesty and possessions, she was overwhelmed (1 Kings 10: 1-9).

Our God can be known; he is not the unreachable end of a ceaseless search. Through Jesus Christ we can have real communion with God as a real person. A unitarian God (who is one and not three) cannot be known at a personal level, but our triune God can be known because he provides for our knowledge of himself through his Son and with the motivation of the Holy Spirit.

When we see God as a Trinity we have all we need to stimulate feelings of awe. C.S. Lewis said that one of the reasons he believed in Christianity was that it is a religion you could not have guessed. Who could have guessed, or worked out with reason or research that God is one being in three distinct persons? We can deduce the doctrine from Scripture, and we can clarify it by contrasting it with heresies that obscure either the distinction of the persons or the unity of God's being. But when we have done all that, we are left to gasp at the mystery. We may explain the doctrine, but we can only bow in awe and astonishment before the reality.

God is self-sufficient

This leads us to consider the amazing independence and self-sufficiency of God. This was expressed for all time to Moses at the burning bush, when he asked God how he should speak of him to the people of Israel. He wanted to know God's name by which he and the people would understand something about the one they were being called upon to trust and obey:

God said to Moses, "I AM WHO I AM. This is what you are to say to the Israelites; 'I AM has sent me to you'" (Exodus 3: 14).

Moses was in the presence of a sight that perfectly illustrated God's meaning. "Though the bush was on fire it did not burn up" (Exodus 3:2). It was constantly giving out but was never diminished — such is the God whom we worship. This is a wonder to us because we have no experience of anything that is self-perpetuating, self-motivating or self-sufficient. Every part of nature depends on other parts and there is chaos and loss when this balance is disturbed. The richest person in the world depends on the air for his breath, his servants to wait on him and on medicine made by others when he is ill. In the triune God we marvel and wonder that he is dependent on no-one outside himself for life, love, companionship, power, wisdom and all else. Little of this will occur to us before we are converted and none of it can be imagined by followers of sects that try to reduce God into terms of human logic. But when we have been introduced to him through Jesus Christ, the sheer immensity of God, his utter perfection and his total completeness, cause us to bow with even more astonishment in his glorious presence.

Oh, the depth of the riches of the wisdom and knowledge of
    God!
How unsearchable his judgements, and his paths beyond
    tracing out!
Who has known the mind of the Lord?   Or who has been his
    counsellor?
Who has ever given to God, that God should repay him?
For from him and through him and to him are all things. To
    him be the glory for ever! Amen (Romans 11: 33-36).

If we are staggered at the self-sufficiency of God, we will be left quite speechless when once we understand that this God, who needs nothing and no-one outside himself, is willing to talk to people like us, listen to our prayers and involve himself in our needs.

Amazing condescension

Every aspect of God's dealings in grace with sinful people is a cause of wonder. His love, his mercy, his patience, his compassion — if we dwell on these for very long, we will develop a sense of awe in the presence of mystery. A subject rather out of fashion nowadays, is God's condescension. Our forefathers taught and wrote about this, but in these days when we try to eliminate distinctions between classes, condescension has a bad press. There is a rather nauseating attitude of people who regard themselves as superior toward those they see as inferior. They feel it is an offence to their dignity to speak to those they regard as lesser mortals. Even when they help those who are less fortunate, they make such people feel of little value.

But when we think of God's condescension, we see him not as great *but* deigning to come down to our level. We see him as both great *and* stooping down to us. Some great people of this world feel they would be in some way diminished if they gave themselves too much to those *beneath them*. But God's condescension is such that his greatness is magnified by it. Think of the Father's condescension as the Psalmist did:

O LORD, our Lord, how majestic is your name in all the earth! ... When I consider your heavens, the work of your fingers, the moon and the stars, which you have set in place, what is man that you are mindful of him, the son of man that you care for him (Psalm 8:1-4)?

This God, who made everything, who sustains everything, and who knows every star in every galaxy, is willing to identify himself with people like us. He says:

For this is what the high and lofty One says — he who lives for ever, whose name is holy: "I live in a high and holy place, but also with him who is contrite and lowly in spirit … " (Isaiah 57:15).

Nowhere is the Father's condescension more graphically portrayed than in his dealings with the people of Israel:

> It was I who taught Ephraim to walk, taking them by the arms, but they did not realise it was I who healed them. I led them with cords of human kindness, with ties of love; I lifted the yoke from their neck and bent down to feed them (Hosea 11: 3-4).

The hymn writer expressed his amazement like this:

> Yet I may love Thee, too, O Lord,
> Almighty as Thou art,
> For Thou hast stooped to ask of me
> The love of my poor heart.
> (F.W.Faber 1814-63)

There is nothing like this in the whole of human experience — it is unique — it is awesome.

The condescension of the Son

As we would expect, when the Son came into the world he showed the same quality as the Father. His willingness to become man and not to be ashamed to call us brothers (Hebrews 2:11) was in itself a great act of condescension. As Paul wrote of Jesus:

> Who, being in very nature God, did not consider equality with God something to be grasped, but made himself nothing, taking the very nature of a servant (Philippians 2: 6-7).

And John tells us:

> The Word became flesh and lived for a while among us (John 1:14).

Our Lord was not pretending to be human. He lived, spoke, thought and felt as we do — though without sin.

The secret of wholesome condescension is that other people do not feel offended or patronised — they are comfortable even in the presence of greatness. Those around Jesus knew that he was the Master, and yet people brought their children to him and ordinary folk enjoyed his company.

The condescension of the Holy Spirit

The Holy Spirit likewise displays this condescension. Consider the condition of human hearts into which he enters:

> ... out of the heart come evil thoughts, murder, adultery, sexual immorality, theft, false testimony, slander (Matthew 15:19).

We cringe at close encounters with people who nauseate and repel us, but the Holy Spirit deigns, not merely to visit us but to live within us as a "gracious willing Guest". Well might we sing:

> Dear Lord, and shall Thy Spirit rest
> In such a wretched heart as mine?
> Unworthy dwelling! glorious Guest!
> Favour astonishing, divine!
> (Anne Steele 1717-78)

The longer we dwell on this stooping grace of the Father, Son and Holy Spirit, the more we will find ourselves able only to gasp in wonder and admiration.

If we had nothing more, we have seen enough to fill our minds with amazement and to give our imaginations more than enough to work on for a lifetime. But there is much more yet to satiate every appetite for wonders and mysteries, and this aspect of our subject is worth one more chapter.

All praise and thanks to God
The Father now be given,
The Son, and him who reigns
With them in highest heaven -
The one eternal God,
Whom earth and heaven adore;
For thus it was, is now,
And shall be evermore.

(Martin Rinckart 1586 - 1649)

16.
The Trinity and more wonders

It was the habit of believers in Old Testament times to prime the pump of their praise and worship by recalling God's mighty deeds. Here is one example:

> Great is the LORD and most worthy of praise; his greatness
>   no-one can fathom.
> One generation will commend your works to another;
>   they will tell of your mighty acts.
> They will speak of the glorious splendour of your majesty,
>   and I will meditate on your wonderful works.
> They will tell of the power of your awesome works, and I
>   will proclaim your great deeds (Psalm 145: 3-6).

We can surely translate the Psalmist's language into terms of our New Testament understanding of God and his wonders. This subject lends itself, of necessity, to endless exploration; for this reason we can only pick out one or two outstanding examples in addition to those mentioned in our last chapter. For instance, let us think for a few moments of the Christmas story — the Incarnation.

The Incarnation

The endless singing of Christmas carols, in which so often profound words are sung with little or no appreciation of their meaning, can rob us of a sense of wonder and amazement at the coming of God's own Son into the world.

Here was an unbelievable miracle involving the three persons of the Trinity, summed up in the reply of the angel to Mary's question "How will this be, since I am a virgin?":

> The Holy Spirit will come upon you, and the power of the Most High will over-shadow you. So the holy one to be born will be called the Son of God   (Luke 1: 34-35).

No wonder Charles Wesley sang:

> Let earth and heaven combine,
> Angels and men agree,
> To praise in songs divine
> The incarnate Deity;
> Our God contracted to a span,
> Incomprehensibly made man.

We admire and wonder at great human achievements such as scaling high mountains, the display of remarkable skills in sport, great feats of endurance, space exploration and much else that excites our praise, but nothing is to be compared with the eternal God being "incomprehensibly made man".

The Father sent his Son. The Spirit energised the whole operation in and through which the eternal Son of God became a helpless baby. Here is a mystery of mysteries, and we may well ask:

> Who is he in yonder stall,
> At whose feet the shepherds fall —

Our response has to be with the hymn writer:

> 'Tis the Lord! O wondrous story!
> 'Tis the Lord, the King of glory!
> At his feet we humbly fall —
> Crown him! crown him, Lord of all!
>   (Benjamin R. Hanby 1833-1867)

Ours is a sceptical and confused generation that sings carols while it doubts the story. And one reason it doubts the story is that it has very little idea, if any, of the greatness of the triune majesty of whom the angel Gabriel said "nothing is impossible with God" (Luke 1:37).

The great wonder of the incarnation can only be matched by another that is equally staggering.

Both God and Man

The person called Jesus of Nazareth, who walked this earth two thousand years ago, was both God and man in one person. He was not merely a man with some miraculous powers, nor was he God pretending to be a man. He was both God and man.

The quality of his life, his miraculous powers and his glorious resurrection taken together show that he was God. He did not give up his deity when he came into the world. At the same time, he had a genuine human nature. John tells us that "the Word became flesh" (John 1:14), which means, as we have seen, that he not only lived like a man, but actually felt hunger, tiredness and disappointment as we do.

How can this be? How can anyone be equally true God and true man? How could Jesus Christ be, not half God and half man, but truly God and truly man, and yet a whole person? How were his human and divine natures related to each other? Such questions have occupied the minds of scholars down the centuries. We know that the Father retained fellowship with the Son during his life on earth (Matthew 3:17), and that Jesus was filled in full measure with the Holy Spirit (John 3:34). But, in the end, we all have to admit that here is a mystery before which we can only bow in adoration:

Thou art the everlasting Word,
The Father's only Son;
God manifestly seen and heard,
And Heaven's beloved One:
Worthy, O Lamb of God, art Thou,
That every knee to Thee should bow.

(Josiah Conder 1789-1855)

We put up monuments to retain the memory of men and women who are considered to have been outstanding in their field. At this very time (2000 AD) an extensive memorial to Diana, Princess of Wales, is being created to provide a focal point for the homage of thousands of people. All this for a dead heroine! Jesus prayed that his disciples would see his glory (John 17:24). That prayer is in part fulfilled here and now, as, by faith, we see the glory of the greatest wonder in the universe, the living, one and only, God-Man. In heaven we will see him and for ever marvel at him.

What more could there possibly be to excite our sense of wonder and awe? There is at least one more great wonder of wonders for us to glimpse.

A suffering God

Here, perhaps, we approach the greatest mystery of all. Some teachers reject the whole notion of a suffering God, believing that he does not have feelings of joy, grief or pain. When the Bible attributes these feelings to God, such teachers tell us that this is using our language to describe things beyond our understanding.

However, when the Bible tells us that "In all their distress he too was distressed" (Isaiah 63:9), we should surely believe that it means what it says. Not to do so is to rob ourselves of a God who has feelings, and to be left with one who is above us and aloof from us. Also, when we are told "... do not grieve the Holy Spirit of God" (Ephesians 4:30), this has little meaning if the Spirit is not actually hurt by our ungodly conduct.

It is at the cross that all God's great attributes are seen in glorious display, and it is here, too, that the veil is lifted just a little into the mystery of his suffering. We have no difficulty in understanding that the Son of God, as man, suffered at Calvary. He bore the most excruciating physical pain, and over and above that he endured suffering within himself that we cannot even begin to imagine.

But let us also think of the Father. The terms in which the Bible speaks of his giving his one and only Son, are surely designed to give us a glimpse into the Father's heart. Paul speaks of God not sparing his Son (Romans 8:32).Had it been possible he would have spared him. How can we possibly admire a Father who looks on impassively, and unperturbed, while the blood of his only Son is poured out in death? No! It was not like that!

All three persons of the Trinity, the Father, the Son and the Holy Spirit were involved in the sufferings of the cross. The writer to the Hebrews tells us that it was "through the eternal Spirit" that Jesus Christ "offered himself unblemished to God" (9:14). Some scholars think "the eternal Spirit" refers to our Lord's own divine nature, while others take it to mean the Holy Spirit. It is true that Jesus could not have offered a perfect sacrifice without his divine nature, but the natural meaning here seems to be that, as the Holy Spirit enabled Jesus to live a spotless life, so he also enabled him to offer that perfect life as an atoning sacrifice to God.

The involvement of the three persons in the great transaction that took place on Calvary should excite our amazement that God should demonstrate such total commitment to the means of our salvation; it should excite our thankfulness that this involvement ensured that nothing needed was left undone or uncertain; it should excite our confidence in a salvation that rests on the work of the triune God, Father, Son and Holy Spirit.

The Inseparable separated

At the depth of this mystery we hear the cry of Jesus on the cross "My God, my God, why have you forsaken me?" (Matthew 27:46). This is as far as we are allowed to go, but how can we understand it? How can we put it into words? We can only try. This was the great transaction by which our sins are forgiven and we are reconciled to God. At this moment the very being of our triune God was torn by immeasurable pain. The inseparable was separated — love spent itself in an agony of total self-giving. The apostle Peter tells us that — "even angels long to look into these things" (1 Peter 1:12). And shall the angels be dumb with astonishment while we remain unmoved and look elsewhere for feelings of awe and wonder? Here is a mystery beyond all mysteries:

> 'Tis a deep that knows no sounding;
> Who its breadth or length can tell?
> On its glories
> Let my soul for ever dwell.
>
>   (John Kent 1766-1843)

Whenever we are troubled by the pains and distresses of oppressed people in the world, let us remember that the one who is in control is not an unfeeling tyrant, but a God who understands suffering as we can never do:

> There is no place where earth's sorrows
> Are more felt than up in heaven;
>
>   (F.W.Faber 1814-63)

Here then, are just some sights of the mysteries of our faith. Those who have seen the Lord's glory in the things we have discussed, will not be among the seekers for sensational happenings or miraculous demonstrations. We have no need to turn to heretical sects, new age experiments or eastern religions (see Appendix 2) — here we have more than enough to capture heart, mind and soul until we enter the glory.

> Glory be to God the Father,
> Glory be to God the Son,
> Glory be to God the Spirit,
> Great Jehovah, Three in One:
> Glory, glory,
> While eternal ages run!
>
>   (Horatius Bonar 1808-89)

17.
The Trinity and Church Fellowship

A missionary in south India was confronted by a serious division in the little church he had founded. The break in fellowship was caused by the refusal of any of the members to admit responsibility for the disappearance of some church money. When the rift persisted, the missionary announced that he would take no food until the thief owned up. The people knew him well enough to be in no doubt that he would carry out his threat, and very soon the culprit was exposed and dealt with, and fellowship was restored. You might think that this action was excessively drastic, but it would be well if all of us valued the unity of the church to which we belong as highly as did that missionary. Too often we are careless about words and attitudes that needlessly harm the unity of the church and pollute its atmosphere.

The Bible frequently uses the expression "the church of God" (1 Corinthians 1:2; 1 Thessalonians 2:14; 1 Timothy 3:15). It is the great privilege of every local church to represent God to a world that is ignorant of him. This is done, in the main, by preaching, and this is tremendously important. But preaching can easily be undermined by the poor quality of church life. Conversely, it is often the quality of church life that first makes an impact on unbelieving people. It is at this point that we frequently fall short, and most churches need their fellowship to be revitalised. One way in which this can be done is by a new and conscious application of the Trinity to our church life. We need to allow ourselves to be mastered by the fact that God himself is a fellowship of love, and that this love is expressed in mutual appreciation and harmonious activity. This is unity in diversity and has to be worked out in church life with much patience.

Church unity motivated by the Trinity

The New Testament is full of exhortations to Christians to be united and to love each other. Many good reasons are used to back up these appeals. For example, Jesus enforced his command to his disciples to love one another with a reminder of his love for them (John 13:34-35), and Paul called for unity in the church partly because this would give him joy (Philippians 2:2) and mainly because of the example of Jesus Christ (Philippians 2: 2-11). But, on more than one occasion, the motivation is at an even higher level. Paul laid down the requirement for unity to the Ephesians in very clear terms:

> As a prisoner for the Lord, then, I urge you to live a life worthy of the calling you have received. Be completely humble and gentle; be patient, bearing with one another in love. Make every effort to keep the unity of the Spirit through the bond of peace (Ephesians 4: 1-3).

At first the argument is that their conduct should be consistent with the message they believed and preached, but then Paul goes on to show that this message is about God who is Father, Son and Holy Spirit:

> There is one body and one Spirit — just as you were called to one hope when you were called — one Lord, one faith, one baptism; one God and Father of all, who is over all and through all and all in all (Ephesians 4:4-6).

There could not be any greater incentive than this for a church to be united in love. Each member has become a Christian only because of the loving and powerful work of the Holy Spirit bringing them to salvation. He opened their minds to receive the truth about their sinfulness and its consequences. He pointed them to Jesus Christ and made them willing to submit to him in repentance and faith. They were all empowered by the same Spirit to live as Christian disciples. There was but one Spirit upon whom they all depended. Not only have all the members the same spiritual origin, but they all have the same hope of eternal life. They have the same Lord who has loved them and died for them. They are all totally dependent on Jesus Christ for pardon. They were all committed to the same Lord when they were baptised. There is only one Lord and all believers are united in him.

Furthermore, there is but one heavenly Father to whom all believers are reconciled and to whom we all come in prayer and worship. He controls all things and provides for all the needs of the world. At the same time he lives in the hearts of all believers by the Holy Spirit. We are in the same family, and are bound together by the strongest possible ties. God is three. God is one. Our church fellowship must be worthy of such a God.

As always, we find Paul's teaching flowing out of basic principles laid down earlier by our Lord himself. In his longest recorded prayer (John 17), Jesus used his special relationship with the Father to show the essential unity of his people:

> Holy Father, protect them by the power of your name — the name you gave me — so that they may be one as we are one (verse 11). I pray also for those who will believe in me through their message, that all of them may be one, Father, just as you are in me and I am in you (verses 20 & 21). I have given them the glory that you gave me, that they may be one as we are one. I in them and you in me (verses 22 & 23).

In these texts we see that the union within the Trinity is to be the pattern and dynamic of unity among Christians. Of special interest is our Lord's request that "those who will believe in me through their message" will be united with the rest of his people. In the story of the early church we see the big problem of uniting Gentiles with the Jewish believers (Acts 15: 5-21; and Galatians 2:11-16), giving point to our Lord's prayer. Nothing in the world, apart from the gospel, can unite people as diverse as Jews and Gentiles in one body (Ephesians 2: 11-18).

Writing to Gentiles, Paul spells out this unity once again in trinitarian terms:

> ... you are no longer foreigners and aliens, but fellow-citizens with God's people and members of God's household, built on the foundation of the apostles and prophets, with Christ Jesus himself as the chief corner stone. In him the whole building is joined together and rises to become a holy temple in the Lord. And in him you too are being built together to become a dwelling in which God lives by his Spirit (Ephesians 2: 19-22).

Those who are united by faith to Jesus Christ, no matter whether they are Jews or Gentiles, have God as their Father and they are children in his household — his family. Or, to change the picture, they are God's temple in which he lives by his Holy Spirit.

This union of Jews and Gentiles can be matched by the bringing together of people from diverse political backgrounds such as nationalists and unionists in Northern Ireland. The same is happening among people from many different racial groups. We see such people united in local churches all over the world.

We are united to each of the three persons of the Trinity, we are one in them and we must reflect this in our relationship with one another in the churches.

Unity and the Lord's death

The frequency of the themes of love and unity in the New Testament is an indication of what, alas, we know from experience, that members of churches are prone to fail in their fellowship. Even in the early church we can see this happening, as in the church at Corinth. The apostle Paul was obliged to deal with disunity there caused by snobbery and greed that were surfacing even at the Lord's supper (1 Corinthians 11:17-22). It is very instructive to notice how he handles the matter. He does so by reminding them of the way in which Jesus instituted the Lord's supper and the heavy emphasis on his self-giving:

... The Lord Jesus, on the night he was betrayed, took bread, and when he had given thanks, he broke it and said, "This is my body, which is for you; do this in remembrance of me". In the same way, after supper he took the cup, saying, "This cup is the new covenant in my blood; do this, whenever you drink it, in remembrance of me" (1 Corinthians 11:23-25).

The Corinthian members must have surely seen that their pride and selfishness was totally incompatible with our Lord's self-giving. And as we have seen in chapter sixteen, the Father, the Son and the Holy Spirit were united in the agony, shame and self-abasement involved in the great transaction that took place at Calvary.

It is this self-giving and self-effacement that is so basic to unity among church members. The Bible does not merely tell us to love one another, but it gives us unanswerable arguments, compelling reasons and reminders of the spiritual dynamic that comes from our union with the Father, the Son and the Holy Spirit.

Let us not minimise the obstacles to unity among church members. Churches are composed of people from different cultural backgrounds, they have a variety of personalities and temperaments, and there is a broad spread of intellectual ability and attainment. All this variety is compounded by the remains of the old nature in each person.

In this situation we see the grace of God at work triumphing over our failings. We will see many more victories as we submit ourselves to Scripture and to one another. We are one, and we must, therefore, be seen to be so, in our forgiving one another and in our caring concern.

Perhaps the place where our unity in local churches is most tested, is in the area of our working together in Christian service. To this we will turn in our next chapter.

> There is only one God,
> there is only one King,
> there is only one Body —
> that is why we sing:
> Bind us together, Lord,
> bind us together
> with cords which cannot be broken;
> bind us together, Lord,
> bind us together,
> O bind us together with love.
>
> (Bob Gillman)

18.
The Trinity and Christian service

We may have a sound biblical view of the need for unity in church fellowship, and we may talk idealistically about loving one another, but it is when we are thrown together with others in some form of Christian service that all this is put to the test. We may find ourselves working with other Sunday School teachers, youth leaders, members of an evangelistic committee, deacons or elders. In this kind of situation conflicting opinions are bound to arise about what should be done, how it should be done, and who should do it. Then it is all too easy for pride, envy or bitterness to rear their ugly heads. When this happens, discord in the church is not far away.

As we are discovering with great regularity, the Scriptures deal with this matter also in terms of the Trinity. The outstanding passage on the subject is in that part of his first letter to the church at Corinth where Paul is telling them how to deal with spiritual gifts:

> There are different kinds of gifts, but the same Spirit. There are different kinds of service, but the same Lord. There are different kinds of working, but the same God works all of them in all men (1 Corinthians 12: 4-6).

The possession and exercise of spiritual gifts had become a cause of pride and disunity in the Corinthian church. The whole purpose of Paul's words was to underline a number of basic principles:

> 1. All gifts in their great variety are from the Holy Spirit, and therefore should not be a cause of pride, since we only have what we have been given and none of us deserve the least of God's gifts.

2. There is a tremendous variety in the forms of service and in the effectiveness of our service. None of us has a monopoly of spiritual gifts and there is room for each person in the work of the church.

3. It is the same Spirit who is at work in each member. All of us, whatever our place in the church, are subject to the direction of the Lord Jesus Christ as the head of the church, and it is the one God and Father who is at work through the Spirit and the Son.

In the light of this teaching, all of us in Christian service must resist the temptation to self-assertiveness, expecting our ideas to prevail, our gifts to be regarded as the most important, or our efforts to be appreciated above those of others. On the other hand, we must be willing to recognise the gifts God has given us. Some people have a tendency, in the name of humility, to play down their abilities. Such an attitude is commendable so long as it is not carried too far. It is honouring to God to acknowledge, with gratitude, the gifts we have, and to be willing for them to be used within the fellowship of the church.

The solution to all such problems is to take serious note that the Spirit, the Son and the Father are at one in the gifting and directing of the work of the churches, and to try to make that unity visible in all that is done.

Self-effacement

We should remember that the Son was willing to subordinate himself to the Father for the purpose of our salvation. The equality of the Father and the Son is absolutely clear, and yet within that equality the Son was willing to be obedient to the Father's will and purpose:

There is complete other-person-centredness in this relationship of the Father to the Son and of the Son to the Father. The Son does nothing of himself, but as the Father taught him (John 8:28). The same is true of the relationship of the Spirit to the Father and the Son. The Spirit is self-effacing. He does not speak from himself but he takes the things of the Son and shows them to believers; he glorifies Christ (John 16:13-14) ... This is the character of God and this is how creation has been made. We have been created in God's image for relationship and this relationship must be other-person-centred.

(*The Everlasting God*, D.Broughton Knox)

Against this background we are compelled to take yet more seriously Paul's exhortations to believers to submit to each other, for example:

Submit to one another out of reverence for Christ (Ephesians 5:21).
Do nothing out of selfish ambition or vain conceit, but in humility consider others better than yourselves. Each of you should look not only to your own interests, but also to the interests of others (Philippians 2:3-4).

This must apply not only to the relationship between the members of the church but also between them and their leaders. This is made clear in such passages as:

... respect those who work hard among you, who are over you in the Lord and who admonish you. Hold them in the highest regard in love because of their work. Live in peace with each other. (1 Thessalonians 5:12-13; see also Hebrews 13:17).

This does not mean unquestioning subservience, but it does warn us against making life unnecessarily difficult for those who lead us.

The example of the Trinity speaks also to church leaders about their attitude to their members. Even in the exercise of the gift of leadership, there must be an element of submission to fellow leaders, and to those they are trying to lead. Our Lord himself laid down clear instructions:

> ... whoever wants to become great among you must be your servant, and whoever wants to be first must be slave of all (Mark 10: 43-44; see also 1 Peter 5: 1-3).

It is not easy to work out the delicate balance between leadership and submission, or between being a guide and at the same time a slave. In this we need the Lord's wisdom and grace, remembering that success will come as much from what we are as from anything we may do. The writer well remembers a church Bible study in which this subject arose. All were agreed that members should submit to each other and also to their leaders. But then I asked "should I, as your leader, be submissive to you?" There was an embarrassed silence, until one brave soul uttered the classic response "I think you mean to be"!!

So we see that a consideration of the loving and harmonious relationship between the three persons of the Trinity teaches us that Christian service involves the self-effacement of each worker, and our submission in love to each other for Christ's sake.

Decision making

Within this relationship of submission, there has to be order, leadership and a means of making decisions. It is clear that, in the Trinity, equality does not of necessity mean sameness of function, and it is also clear that leaders are appointed in churches for the purpose of making decisions. Without this the result can only be indecision at best and chaos at worst. The effect of insisting on equality without distinction of function is not to create understanding and harmony but the very opposite. Harmony, as in the body (1 Corinthians 12:12-26), flows not from each member copying the other, but from each member functioning as it is intended. Nor is this to say that one member is more important than another, because each is dependent on the others and cannot function properly apart from them.

All this must be applied to the Biblical teaching of the "headship" of men. Once again Paul puts this in the context of the Trinity:

> Now I want you to realise that the head of every man is Christ, and the head of the woman is man, and the head of Christ is God (1 Corinthians 11:3).

The meaning of the word "head" in this verse is understood by some people as meaning "source" — woman derives her being from man. This meaning can hardly be applied to "the head of Christ is God", but even if we accept it, the subordination of women to men in church life, in an atmosphere of partnership and mutual respect, is clear.

One aim

The three persons of the Trinity are united in love and purpose, and that purpose is the glory of God the Father. Paul spells this out in a remarkable passage:

> ... the end will come, when he (Jesus Christ) hands over the kingdom to God the Father ... then the Son himself will be made subject to him who put everything under him, so that God may be all in all (1 Corinthians 15:24-28; see also Philippians 2:11).

This also has to be the aim and object of all Christian service. We want many blessings in the life of the church and we want others to be saved and united to God's people. But if these objectives become ends in themselves, we have lost our way, and we are no longer trinitarian people.

When we have this motive clearly in mind, then it is most likely that tensions and divisions will be nullified, and loving unity like that of our blessed God himself will prevail.

Lord of the church,
   we seek a Father's blessing,
a true repentance and a faith restored,
a swift obedience and a new possessing,
filled with the Holy Spirit of the Lord[3]
We turn to Christ
   from all our restless striving
unnumbered voices
   with a single prayer —
the living water for our souls' reviving,
in Christ to live,
   and love and serve and care.

                 (Timothy Dudley-Smith)

19.
The Trinity and revival

It is obvious to all spiritually minded people that, for the most part in the western world, these are days of spiritual barrenness. It is true that there are some places where more people are being converted than in others and where churches are growing in spiritual health and vitality. But even in such places people with understanding realise that they are not experiencing spiritual revival.

Revival is not easy to describe, but the best we can say is that when it occurs, the presence of God makes such an impact on churches that they become "saturated with God". The effect of this is first in the churches themselves in terms of heart-searching followed by joy in the Lord, and then in the community at large with many conversions and a moral cleansing of society. We long for revival. For this reason it is possible, in desperation, to entertain wrong ideas about how revival comes to us and what we should do about it. Once again the great fact of the Trinity is a sure guide.

Confirmation of our evangelical faith

The first thing to observe is that revival only ever comes in the context of the evangelical faith and always promotes it. By the evangelical faith we mean belief in the authority of Scripture, the substitutionary atonement, the need for regeneration, justification by faith only and the personal return of Jesus Christ. Commitment to these vital truths is always stronger in and after a time of revival.

This is a tremendous confirmation of our position as evangelicals, giving it the highest possible approval — that of God himself.

It is significant that revival has never come to churches of a liberal persuasion (those who deny the great Bible truths we have just mentioned). Such churches do sometimes adopt charismatic ideas and practices, but this is not the same as experiencing God-sent revival. Furthermore, God has not visited Unitarian churches (those who deny that God is a Trinity) with a spiritual awakening.

The fact that revivals occur only among evangelical churches puts the seal of God's confirmation both on the evangelical faith as a whole, and, by implication, on the doctrine of the Trinity in particular. Nothing could be more encouraging.

Intensified Experience

A major effect of revival is the intensifying of what otherwise may be described as the normal way in which God works. This, yet again, underlines the triunity of God. He comes to his people in the person and power of the Holy Spirit, and the Scripture teaches us that one of the great works of the Spirit is to convince us that we have sinned against God:

> When he comes, he will convict the world of guilt in regard
> to sin and righteousness and judgement (John 16:8).

In the normal way, for the most part, we are made aware of our sinfulness at sufficient depth to make us realise that something has to be done about it. Sometimes tears are shed, but rarely is there a great display of emotion. In contrast, one of the great characteristics of a time of revival is a deep agonising of soul under the terrible awareness of the judgement of God on our sin. This not only affects individual people, but whole congregations break down in a trauma of conviction and confession. This sometimes lasts for long periods of time. We have an example of this in the time of Nehemiah in Old

Testament days. There came a time when he and his colleagues had to exhort the people to be joyful, "for all the people had been weeping as they listened to the words of the Law" (Nehemiah 8:9). Unconverted people are humbled before God by revival, but so also are people who are already Christians. There is an intensification of their sense of guilt and unworthiness such as they have not experienced before. This conviction of sin sooner or later gives way to peace with God through our Lord Jesus Christ. This is the Spirit's work:

... he will testify about me (John 15:26).
He will bring glory to me by taking from what is mine and making it known to you. All that belongs to the Father is mine. That is why I said the Spirit will take from what is mine and make it known to you (John 16:14-15).

The Spirit uses the ministry of the Word to bring about this turning to Christ which results in great joy (1 Thessalonians 1: 5-6). This exuberance is shared by the whole community and becomes a focus of attention for churches around and the community at large. The churches take on a new image of vitality and boldness.

How do revivals come?

This leads us to ask the urgent questions, how do revivals come, and what can we do about it? It is here that what we have seen so far helps us to avoid mistakes. The biggest mistake that many people make in their earnest and sincere longing for revival is this, they assume that it is possible to lay down a programme of things we can do that will guarantee the outpouring of the Spirit. The idea is that if we create the right conditions, God will respond with revival blessing. But revival is from God the Father and the Son, sending the Holy Spirit to his people. This should teach us two things. One is that revival is a sovereign gift of God that we cannot possibly order or command. Indeed, if there is a condition above others that would bring revival, it would be the humbling of ourselves before God in confession and admission that we are not able to do anything to merit his coming and that we are unworthy that he should do so.

The second lesson is undoubtedly the need for prayer for revival. It is the united conclusion of all who have studied the history of revivals that these have been most often, if not always, preceded by the earnest and united prayers of God's people. This is certainly in harmony with God's promise:

> If my people, who are called by my name, will humble them-
> selves and pray and seek my face and turn from their wicked
> ways, then will I hear from heaven and will forgive their sin
> and will heal their land (2 Chronicles 7:14).

But, let us beware of using prayer for revival as an excuse for doing nothing. Some dear people have concluded that there is nothing for us to do but to pray: they forget that our Lord has not withdrawn his commission to us to preach the gospel throughout the world. We do not know if God will send another revival, or if he does when this might be, but we do know that our business is to be faithful to his commands.

The place was shaken

Let us see how this worked out in the early church. There was a moment when the Spirit came upon them:

> After they prayed, the place where they were meeting was
> shaken. And they were all filled with the Holy Spirit and
> spoke the word of God boldly (Acts 4:31).

What were the circumstances in which the Holy Spirit was given in such measure? It would be quite right to say that this was in response to the prayers of believers united in heart and mind before the Lord. This is the normal pattern, and pleading for revival should be a constant theme in our private prayers and in our church prayer meetings.

However, we do well to observe a number of important things about this situation. The first is that they did not ask directly for the outpouring of the Spirit as such, but that the sovereign God would intervene in their situation:

> Sovereign Lord ... You spoke by the Holy Spirit through the mouth of your servant, our father David: "Why do the nations rage and the peoples plot in vain? The kings of the earth take their stand and the rulers gather together against the Lord and against his Anointed One." Indeed Herod and Pontius Pilate met together with the Gentiles and the people of Israel in this city to conspire against your holy servant Jesus ... Now, Lord, consider their threats and enable your servants to speak your word with great boldness. Stretch out your hand to heal and perform miraculous signs ... (Acts 4:24-30).

The second thing to note is that they had been, and continued to be, occupied with gospel work for which they were now suffering. Their prayers were in the context of faithful preaching and witnessing. Thirdly, the blessing they sought was not for themselves as such, but for the advancing of Christ's kingdom. Finally, their work and their prayers were clearly directed to the honouring of the Father and the Son. According to this pattern, it is when we are actively engaged in gospel work with a view to honouring the Father and the Son, that the Holy Spirit comes down in power. At the same time let us pray:

> Oh, that you would rend the heavens and come down, that the mountains would tremble before you! ... Since ancient times no-one has heard, no ear has perceived, no eye has seen any God besides you, who acts on behalf of those who wait for him (Isaiah 64: 1 & 4).

Great Father of mercies,
Thy goodness I own,
And the covenant love
Of thy crucified Son;
All praise to the Spirit,
Whose whisper divine
Seals mercy, and pardon,
And righteousness mine.

(John Stocker b.1776)

20.
The Trinity and our inheritance

Most of the people around us are uncertain as to the purpose of their lives and even more vague about their eternal destiny. A doctor, Garth Wood, writing in the Daily Telegraph on the 15th November, 1997 said "We wait nervously for death, that endless nothingness at the end of brief being". It is very likely that the majority of his readers would think much the same. The effect of this lack of hope on society is obvious. As Paul wrote, reflecting the common attitude of the people of his day:

> ... if the dead are not raised, let us eat and drink, for tomorrow we die (1 Corinthians 15:32).

One of the main reasons for confusion and lawlessness in society today is the widespread uncertainty, and even downright unbelief, about the life to come. Nothing breeds carelessness more effectively than hopelessness.

In the light of this hopelessness in the world at large, Christians have a great privilege. We have a glorious future that has been secured for us, and our certainty about it rests on the work of Father, Son and Holy Spirit. We will be brought at last into eternal glory to share forever in the love, peace and purity of God's presence. This is the completion of the work planned by the Father, put into operation by the Son and brought to its desired conclusion by the Holy Spirit:

> ... being confident of this, that he who began a good work in you will carry it on to completion until the day of Christ Jesus (Philippians 1:6).

We see this clearly worked out in Paul's writings. For example he wrote to the Galatian believers:

> ... when the time had fully come, God sent his Son, born of a woman, born under law, to redeem those under law, that we might receive the full rights of sons. Because you are sons, God sent the Spirit of his Son into our hearts, the Spirit who calls out, "Abba, Father". So you are no longer a slave, but a son; and since you are a son, God has made you also an heir (Galatians 4:4-7).

Here we see clearly that the Father initiated the work of our salvation and sent his Son into the world to provide for our rescue from sin and its consequences. The Spirit makes this real to us and enables us to enter into a relationship with God as his children. This in turn ensures that we are heirs of God, and like children adopted by rich parents we are entitled to a share in the family fortune.

The apostle Paul gives us a similar scenario in his letter to the Roman Christians:

> For you did not receive a spirit that makes you a slave again to fear, but you received the Spirit of sonship. And by him we cry, "Abba, Father". The Spirit himself testifies with our spirit that we are God's children. Now if we are children, then we are heirs — heirs of God and co-heirs with Christ, if indeed we share in his sufferings in order that we may also share in his glory (Romans 8: 15-17).

Because of all Jesus Christ has done for us, the Father receives us as his children and we are therefore his heirs.

The certainty of this inheritance is made clear to us in this passage when Paul says "heirs of God and co-heirs with Christ". Here are two facts; first that Jesus Christ has an inheritance, and second that believers are heirs with him. The inheritance that Christ received is called "his glory" (Luke 24:26). The writer to the Hebrews tells us that the Son was "appointed heir of all things" (Hebrews 1:2). Wonder of wonders we share that glory with him! This is possible because when we come to faith in Jesus Christ, this faith unites us to him, so that from then onward what is true of him is also true of us. We are united to Christ in his death, burial and resurrection (Romans 6:4-6). We are also, by faith, joined to him in his ascension and entry into glory, as Paul says:

> Praise be to the God and Father of our Lord Jesus Christ, who has blessed us in the heavenly realms with every spiritual blessing in Christ (Ephesians 1:3).

This is our present position in Christ:

> You died, and your life is now hidden with Christ in God (Colossians 3:3),

and this present position guarantees our future entry into glory. As Paul continued:

> When Christ, who is your life, appears, then you also will appear with him in glory (Colossians 3:4).

We see then that our entry into glory is as certain as Christ's entry. Just as he received the inheritance, so we, who are united with him, will without doubt share it with him. We are co-heirs with Christ. We should never forget that we will enjoy our eternal inheritance as whole people, body as well as soul. The end scene will not be heaven, into which we enter when we die. When Jesus Christ returns he will usher in the new heaven and new earth about which Peter wrote (2 Peter 3:13). At that time our bodies will be raised. Paul tells us about that:

> And if the Spirit of him who raised Jesus from the dead is living in you, he who raised Christ from the dead will also give life to your mortal bodies through his Spirit, who lives in you (Romans 8:11).

Once again we see that the three persons of the Trinity are involved in this work. The Father is going to raise us from the dead, and he is going to do this by the Holy Spirit. If we add to this the words of Jesus we find that Jesus himself will do it:

> For my Father's will is that everyone who looks to the Son
> and believes in him shall have eternal life, and I will raise
> him up at the last day (John 6:40).

Just as the three persons were all concerned with the beginning of
our salvation and the continuation of the work of grace within us, so
all three members of the Trinity will see the work to its conclusion.

> Our God is the Lord of life and death, of time and eternity,
> of past, present and future. What he did for Christ he will do
> for us because we share the same indwelling Spirit ... we
> look to the day of glory when we shall know as we are known,
> giving praise that is justly due to Father, Son, and Holy
> Spirit, one God, blessed forever.
> (*The Triune God,* Samuel J. Mikolaski)

What will our future life be like? What will occupy our minds for all
eternity? The subject has to be vast enough and substantial enough
to remain undiminished by eternal contemplation. No such theme
exists apart from the triune God himself. In this book we have reminded ourselves of an enjoyment that begins here and now, and
that will be our never ending delight in the life to come.

> The whole triumphant host
> Give thanks to God on high:
> Hail, Father, Son, and Holy Ghost!
> They ever cry.
> Hail, Abraham's God and mine!
> I join the heavenly lays;
> All might and majesty are Thine,
> And endless praise.
> (Thomas Olivers, 1725-99)

Appendix 1:
Aids to Faith

God has made himself known in what he has made (Psalm 19:1 and Romans 1:19-20), and his character is reflected in his handiwork. This being so it would be very surprising if his triune nature were not in some way stamped on his creation. If we had no evidence of this we might have reason to wonder whether our understanding of God as a Trinity is correct.

Happily, we can see the evidence quite clearly, but we must be careful how we use it. We must never claim that there are proofs of the Trinity to be found in the world. All we can do is point to the remarkable frequency in which combinations of three occur in the world. However, none of these examples that we will quote have the characteristic of three distinct things that are nevertheless one — an indivisible whole. They are not trinitarian.

We receive the teaching that God is a triune being on the evidence of Scripture alone, but it is encouraging to see "threeness" reflected in things all around us. For instance the very structure of space is in threes: space is measured in breadth, length and height; natural life forms can be either animal, vegetable or mineral; time is divided into past, present and future.

Human beings, made in the image of God, have this same tendency. There have been a number of ways in which the human personality has been understood, of which the best known "triples" are "mind, knowledge and love" — "memory, intelligence and will" — and "mind, desires and will". These and others are discussed in *The Doctrine of God*, Herman Bavinck.

Bavinck also draws attention to some triples in Scripture, such as mankind being divided among Noah's three sons, Shem, Ham and Japheth, or the tabernacle division into three parts, the outer court, the holy place and the holy of holies.

We may also find "threeness" in the religious feelings and longings of people generally. Some hanker for a transcendent being, above the world and in sovereign control of all things. Others desire to feel a divine being near to them, comforting, strengthening and guiding them. Others look within themselves for a god who will give joy, peace and satisfaction. World religions tend to emphasise one or other of these cravings of the human soul. It is the glory of the Christian faith that in the triune God we have one who is transcendent, yet near to us and within us. He alone can completely satisfy the needs of his creatures.

All these things are interesting but as Bavinck says:

> ... not any of these analogies nor all of them together can prove the divine Trinity; for that doctrine we are dependent wholly on Scripture. Nevertheless, these illustrations serve to prove that belief in the divine Trinity is not absurd or unreasonable. (*The Doctrine of God*, Banner of Truth)

Appendix 2:
The uniqueness of the Trinity

At the present time Christianity is being thought of more and more as but one religion out of many, and of no greater significance than others. School children are taught to take as much interest in other religions as in Christianity, and sometimes Christianity is compared unfavourably with other faiths.

It is important to respect the traditions, opinions and experiences of others. We must be foremost advocates of freedom of conscience, and abhor every semblance of persecution or physical violence against followers of non-Christian religions. People who resort to oppressive laws and practices to prevent conversions from their followers to other faiths only demonstrate the weakness of their own position.

This said, we must declare, as strongly as we possibly can, that Christianity is different, totally apart from others and irreconcilably incompatible with them. This can be shown in many ways. For example, Christianity alone offers eternal blessings entirely and only on the basis of faith to the complete exclusion of human effort. In every other religion its followers must earn whatever benefit is held out to them.

But the place where the distinction is most clearly seen is in the doctrine of the Trinity. As Dr. D.M.Lloyd-Jones said:

Do we realise, I wonder, as we should, that the doctrine of the Trinity is in a sense the essence of the Christian faith? It is this doctrine which, of all others, differentiates the Christian faith from every other faith whatsoever. (On Ephesians 2:18)

This may surprise some people because they have been told that many other religions have their "trinities" and that therefore Christianity is not unique. Professor Herman Bavinck, in his great work *The Doctrine of God*, agrees that the number three is prominent in other religions. But after listing some examples he says:

> But inasmuch as all these analogies are polytheistic it is difficult to connect them with the Christian doctrine of the Trinity.

In other words, while others may have a threesome of principles or deities, none of them has a divine being who is three persons in one God. They are triads, not trinities. This is not a quibble about words, or a distinction without a difference. The two positions are worlds apart. The idea that Christianity borrowed its doctrine from other religions is ludicrous. The idea that the beliefs of other religions are distortions of the Christian faith is unproven, but much more likely. The doctrine of the Trinity comes from nowhere except the Bible, as D. Broughton Knox makes clear:

> The Trinity is not a concept that the human mind can arrive at from its own resources. It is an historical fact that this doctrine has never occurred to anyone in any of the religions of the world outside the Christian revelation.
> (*The Everlasting God*, Evangelical Press)

It is very strange that anyone in his or her right mind would want to exchange our God for any other. Let Joshua's challenge stand for all time:

> ... if serving the Lord seems undesirable to you, then choose for yourselves this day whom you will serve, whether the gods your forefathers served beyond the River, or the gods of the Amorites, in whose land you are living. But as for me and my household, we will serve the Lord (Joshua 24:15).

Joshua would say to people today, reject Christianity if you will, but your problem will be to choose what you will put in its place. Every alternative in world religions, religious sects, or humanistic ideas is without substance, strength or satisfaction compared with Christianity centred in the triune God, Father, Son and Holy Spirit. This is our God!

Appendix 3:
The Doctrine of the Trinity

Here are two formal statements of the doctrine of the Trinity. Human understanding is limited, and consequently human language is inadequate. We have to do the best we can.

The Baptist Confession of Faith (1689)

In this divine and infinite Being there are three subsistences, the Father, the Word or Son, and Holy Spirit, of one substance, power, and eternity, each having the whole divine essence, yet the essence undivided: the Father is of none, neither begotten nor proceeding; the Son is eternally begotten of the Father; the Holy Spirit proceeding from the Father and the Son; all infinite, without beginning, therefore but one God, who is not to be divided in nature and being, but distinguished by several peculiar relative properties and personal relations; which doctrine of the Trinity is the foundation of all our communion with God, and comfortable dependence on him.
(1 John 5:7; Matt.28:19; 2 Cor.13:14; Exod.3: 14; John 14:11; 1 Cor.8:6; John 1:14,18; John 15:26; Gal. 4:6).

A Baptist affirmation of Faith (1966)

United in the one essence of God there are three persons, the Father, the Son and the Holy Spirit. These are distinct persons since the Father is not the Son and not the Holy Spirit, and the Son is not the Holy Spirit. Each of these persons possesses the entire divine essence undivided, and therefore the perfections which belong to God belong to each of the three persons.

The Father is of none, neither begotten nor proceeding; the Son is eternally begotten of the Father; the Holy Spirit is eternally proceeding from the Father and the Son.
(Matt.3: 16-17; 28:19; 2 Cor. 13:14; 1 John 5:7; John 14:26; Psa.90:2; John 1:14 and 18; 8:42; 16:28; 15:26).

Bibliography

The Three Are One	Stuart Olyott	Evangelical Press 1979
Shared Life	Donald Macleod	Scripture Union 1987
The Everlasting God	D.Broughton Knox	Evangelical Press 1982
Understanding the Trinity	Alister McGrath	Kingsway Publications 1987
Jesus and the World Religions	Ajith Fernando	Marc 1987
Knowing God	J.I.Packer	Hodder & Stoughton 1973
The Trinity in a Pluralistic Age	Ed. Kevin J. Vanhoozen	Eerdmans 1997
Worship, Community and the Triune God of Grace	James B. Torrance	Paternoster Press 1996
The Doctrine of God	Herman Bavinck	Banner of Truth 1977
Equality but not Symmetry	Michael Ovey	Cambridge Papers Vol. 1 No. 2 1992

The Human Identity Crises	Michael Ovey	Cambridge Papers Vol. 4 No. 2 1995
What happens when I pray?	N. R. Needham & D. Harman	Grace Publications Trust 1997 (Great Christian Classics)
Living with the Living God	Owen & Smeaton	Grace Publications Trust 1997 (Great Christian Classics)
The Trinity	E.H.Bickersteth	Kregel
Communion with God	Owen, abridged by R.J.K.Law	Banner of Truth 1991

By the same author

Born Slaves	Grace Publications
Only Servants	Grace Publications
Jeremiah	Geneva Bible Notes
The Beauty of Jesus	Grace Publications
Our Father	Grace Publications
For Starters	Grace Publications
Great Expectations	Grace Baptist Mission — its recent history

Some recent Grace Publications titles

Aspects of Holiness — Bishop J C Ryle — Great Christian Classics No. 20
> Studies in the nature and practice of biblical holiness

How can I be sure? — Revd Frank Allred
> A study of the nature of biblical assurance of salvation

The triumph of Grace — Dr N R Needham
> Extracts from the writings of Augustine of Hippo on the grace of God in our salvation.

2000 years of Christ's power Vol. 1 — Dr N R Needham
> The age of the early Christian Fathers

2000 years of Christ's power Vol. 2 — Dr N R Needham
> The Middle Ages

A full catalogue of Grace Publication titles can be obtained from:

Mr David Kingdon
115 Heritage Park
St Mellons
CARDIFF CF3 ODS
England

Grace Publications titles under preparation

Baptism - the sign and seal of grace — Brian Russell
    The Bible teaching about believers' baptism explained

The life of God in the soul of Man — Scougal
    Another title in the Great Christian Classic series

Autumn gold — Clifford Pond
    Christian preparation for a good old age

2000 years of Christ's power Vol. 3 — Dr N R Needham
    The Reformation period